# THE RAPE NEST

## JACK REYNOLDS

PUBLISHED BY FIDELI PUBLISHING, INC.

© Copyright 2016, Jack Reynolds

All rights reserved.

No part of this book may be reproduced, stored in a retrieval system, or transmitted by any means, electronic, mechanical, photocopying, recording, or otherwise, without written permission from the author.

ISBN: 978-1-60414-940-1

# An overview of *The Rape Nest*

Little Sissy Williams' life had become a pattern of rape and molestation. Unlike many five year olds, she was aware that what was being done to her was evil and wrong. What she never understood was why.

Many times, after her father or her father's friend completed violations, she found comfort by acknowledging the presence of· her guardian angels. They nurtured her soul and kept her mind whole and hopeful. As a child with protective instincts, she also took it upon herself to protect her angels from the chance of being hurt by her two lifelong abusers.

The angels, Ozz and Chism, were perhaps imaginary, but to her and the many who read her story, they become not only possibilities but a salvation strong enough to stand up to the evil acts of men who destroy the innocence of children.

Ozz and Chism are torn between the rules of heaven concerning intervention and the love of a child, who they feel is entitled to protection. With their hands ultimately tied by supreme forces, the angels revert to the use of two compassionate human heroes as tools to intervene and ultimately end little Sissy's constant torment.

Those doing her wrong are finally confronted, and Sissy's imaginary protector become a reality. For the rapist to simply die would have been an injustice. They deserved and received the horrifying sting of death.

In truth, many sexual predators die of natural causes but their demise in *The Rape Nest* is as it should be for all that violate the sacred rights of children.

Jack Thomas Reynolds<br>
e-mail: Reynoldsjackt@aol.com

# PROLOGUE

This is a story based upon the memories of an African American woman who made it through many nights of sexual abuse. She had no savior. She had no heroes to turn to. She had no knight in shining armor. The only prayer answered was that she made it through each night alive.

Throughout her childhood, she believed she had a guardian angel. Her angel was there only to comfort her while she was alone and not to fight or stop her attackers. She imagined this guardian as her only true friend.

All of the incidents of child rape written about in this story actually occurred. Her father and her mother's male lover sexually assaulted little Sissy Williams. The assaults began at age four and continued until she was well past her ninth birthday. Most of the assaults occurred in her own bed, as her mother slept in the very next room. The hopelessness, loneliness, fear and the nightly frustrations were also real.

Her mother claimed she had no idea what was going on and that she was never made aware of the assaults. Ironically, Sissy's mother was only twelve years old when she married her father, Henry, who was 46.

The horrendous nights the child endured at the hands of her deceptively loving father were as cruel and violent as the rape of vengeance by her father's friend. To believe that these two men weren't aware of each other's acts would be ludicrous. To suspect for a moment that the mother was completely unaware of the rape nest in her own home would also be asinine.

In this story, the unexplainable surge of sexual assaults upon children, cause the Earth Angel named Ozz to be assigned to watch over the abused and to assess the reasons behind the attacks. After witnessing these atrocities nightly, Ozz becomes emotionally attached to his subjects and begins to defy the no-interference rule.

PART ONE

# THE RAPE NEST

# CHAPTER 1

"Come here, little girl," he said and patted his leg. "Sit on Floyd's lap."

Floyd sat with a towel lying across his lap and his feet soaking in a pan of hot water in a dark and dirty trucking warehouse. "Come here," he said in a stronger tone. "Your momma said you were gonna treat Floyd right. I've got something for you and a little package for your momma that's really going to make her happy. Come over here, you pretty little thing."

Floyd was what some folks would call a handsome man. He had just turned thirty-three in the month of August. He had brown skin, unusually fine hair and dark piercing eyes shadowed by heavy eyebrows. His pearly white teeth remained in view even when he wasn't smiling. His face was smooth and blemish free. Seldom was he seen without a cigarette in hand. And he had enough charisma to sweep the finest of women off their feet with just one glance. When Floyd looked into a mirror, what he saw was an extremely handsome face.

The small five-year-old black girl was frightened by the mere size of the huge warehouse with all of its dreary, unending ceilings. Floyd was now looking over his sunglasses with a demanding look.

"Come here, I said. You're making Uncle Floyd angry just standing there."

Little Sissy Williams looked up at the man calling himself her uncle. He was now blowing on a small pinwheel tow that swirled with colors with each breath.

"Do you want this special little toy?" he asked.

Sissy didn't say a word, but the spinning wind toy was captivating to her. She reached out her hand without taking a single step.

"No, you gotta come and get it," he said. "Floyd's not gonna hurt you. Come on now, come over here and get it. It's yours."

Sissy remained exactly where she was but kept her eyes focused on the toy. She wondered how it spun around with just a short puff of air. She reached out again, wanting to hold the toy and try it herself.

"Oh, well," he said, "I guess you don't want it." He stopped puffing on the toy and put it on the floor near the base of the old worn out couch he was sitting on.

He continued soaking his feet while glancing at the child occasionally to see if she was giving in to the temptation of the toy. Sissy stood fast and began to look around the room. She had no idea why she was here or why her momma sent her instead of one of her older brothers.

"Damn it, Sissy, get over here! Don't make me have to tell your momma."

Little Sissy, now frightened by the tone of Floyd's voice began to quietly cry. She wiped her eyes as she slowly walked towards the man. Floyd waited calmly as she came within his reach.

"Got-cha!" he said as he grabbed her by the arm.

He violently pulled her onto his lap and began immediately to kiss her on her cheek, then got bolder and kissed the child's lips. The whole time, he was making sounds like he was sampling a delicious food.

Little Sissy turned her head from side to side in an effort to avoid his nasty breath and to gasp for air as his lips prevented her from breathing. Floyd was squeezing her so tight she was beginning to feel faint. He continued to moan and progress in his abuse. Eventually the child sat on his naked lap in a state of shock. Floyd proceeded to please himself in every way his sick mind could think of until he was finally exhausted. Floyd sat smiling with fulfillment like a beast that had just tortured and devoured its helpless prey.

Sissy began to return to her senses. Her navy blue cotton dress with laced shoulder straps was on the floor. It had been stretched and torn in Floyd's frenzy to get it off her. Her underpants were tucked under his thigh.

Floyd finally fell asleep, allowing Sissy a chance to free herself and climb down off his lap. She quickly put her dress on over her small bruised body and left her underclothes where they were. She slowly backed away from Floyd and bravely, grabbed the bag from the nearby table and ran toward the exit door.

In nearly total darkness Sissy attempted to open the door. She turned the knob both ways and pulled, but it would not open. Floyd mumbled and rolled to his side as if he were getting up off the couch. After glancing back at Floyd, who was in a sleepy daze and looking directly at her, she continued to try and escape. A bolt lock far above her reach was latched tightly. Realizing she was trapped, she slumped to the floor and quietly began cry again. She was afraid that he would do it again when he woke up.

After a while, she managed to get back up onto her feet and with all her might attempted to open the door. Without ceasing her effort to escape, she turned to make sure that Floyd had fallen back to sleep.

Suddenly the door was unlatched from above. A tall black man, who had witnessed Floyd's acts, lifted her up with one arm and pulled the door open with the other. He moved quickly out of the warehouse and onto the street. Sissy was clinging tightly to him and looking over his shoulder to see if Floyd was coming after her. The man carried her for a few blocks without so much as a word. Little Sissy continued to cling to his shirt, as the warehouse seemed to fade further and further into the dark distance.

The man who had rescued her turned into a vacant house. After climbing a flight of steps to the second floor he sat her down and looked out the front window to see if anyone had followed them. He looked in both directions and walked to the other side of the room and looked out that way too. When he was satisfied no one had followed them, he bolted the door. After returning to the front window he nervously looked out again to see if anyone had seen him enter the house.

Sissy was standing exactly where he had put her down. She too wanted to know if Floyd had followed. Was she safe from him or would he at any moment burst through the door and take her back?

As the man relaxed and eased up his vigilance, Sissy walked over to him as he still peered out the window. She leaned against his leg where she felt that she was finally safe.

In the darkness with only the light from an outside streetlight she stood motionless for nearly another hour as the man continued to glance outside and occasionally down at her. He had yet to speak.

In the dimly lit room in complete silence he finally backed away from the window and sat on a pile of old clothing. Sissy stood on her toes for one more assuring glance that Floyd could not find them. Hurt and exhausted she walked over to her savior who was now lying down.

She sat down beside him as he placed his finger to his lips in a gesture for her to be quiet. The man hugged and gently kissed her on the forehead. She was safe. She had gotten away.

Sissy cautiously cuddled up to him. Lying in the shadows of this deteriorated room with all of its peeling paint and cracked plaster, she looked out through the broken window. The bright stars of the night were sparkling above as if all were right with the world. She wondered if her guardian angel had somehow turned into this man and come to rescue her.

She wondered what would happen next. She yearned to be home with her brothers, even though being there would not protect her from Floyd or her father. Tired, worn-out and depleted she began to doze off.

Her newly found hero had hidden on an upper deck of the warehouse during the day with the intention of stealing whatever he could once everyone had gone for the night. He had accidentally fallen asleep for several hours before being awakened by the loud sexual sounds made by Floyd as he attacked the small child. He quietly witnessed the incident with the initial hope that they would hurry it up and leave, allowing him to proceed with his intended theft.

As he watched, he found himself becoming unexpectedly aroused at the sight of this six-foot man steadily pounding himself against the small young girl. Even at a distance, he could see the man's expression of ecstasy as his eyes rolled back into his head with each thrust. "Oh, Jesus!" he loudly blurted out with each heightened level of violent pleasure. The child lay silent and yielded to every push with her tearful eyes wide open.

Now as he was lying next to her, he was beginning to feel a powerfully driven madness to fulfill his own sexual needs. He casually managed to get his hand down onto the child's bare legs just above her knees while attempting not to awaken her. Slowly he began to move his hand from thigh to thigh at first squeezing gently and then harder and harder.

"No," Sissy said as she began to awaken. He, like every other adult male in her life, ignored her and continued to force himself upon her. This time, Sissy did not even whimper. She'd thought for a moment that her pleas had been answered, only to find that she was again caught in the same web.

The eyes that watched from above this time were filled with fury. So many times he had watched as men fell to the forbidden temptation of violating children. So many times he had to patiently wait until they completed their acts before he could go to the child's side. Again and again and again, year after year, place after place, child after child, the angel known as Ozz had held his anger inside and helplessly yielded to the laws that govern Heaven and Earth.

These laws said he must submit to the ignorance and arrogance of evil. The pain caused by the restraints that bound him had ruptured his soul. On one hand, his love for mankind had fallen below his God-given expectations, but on the other hand, it had triggered his natural desire to protect the innocent.

The man on Hamilton Avenue had pawed over Sissy's near lifeless body. He kissed, fondled and sexually abused her just as Floyd had. The acts of this deceiver were as evil as Floyd's, who she had learned to both, hate and fear.

Ozz was suffering inside. Once again he had to helplessly stand by, against his own will, while a precious young child suffered the merciless pains of rape — a child who had called upon him, as her guardian angel, to watch over her and to make her mother love her. *What a small request,* Ozz had thought.

"I don't understand," he said to his own recently appointed archangel. "Among the thousands of voices that cry out to God, this child's voice has been filled with distress beyond even my imagination. Why am I expected to stand idly by because intervention would take away the rights of evil to exist? Is this some kind of statement of Good and Evil created by God? Is evil just as sacred as good?" Ozz was pacing as he paused and looked directly into the eyes of his fellow guardian angel and waited for a response.

"You are aware, as well as I, that our only involvement is to comfort and nurture their spirits," the second angel said.

"Most children don't even know they have a spirit. The root of all evil is tormenting this child. This desire to inflict dominance and cruelty upon a helpless child is nothing less than satanic. There must be something that I can do."

"What is it that you would like to do?" asked Chism, the second angel.

"I am seething with anger. I'll tell you ... I'll tell you exactly what I'd like to do," Ozz responded.

Though Ozz's life spanned many years, he had been an Earth Angel for less than fifty human years. The role of comforting the souls of children that have reached a potentially devastating level of distress was a stage-one assignment that could lead Ozz to a higher rank of Archangel. The much sought after advancement was contingent upon the angel's ability to lift the spirits of brokenhearted children, and prevent them from spiraling into a life of hopeless despair.

Until now, Ozz had been at the top of his sector. However, a recent onslaught of certain evils had introduced a new awareness of predatory humans to him. This particular generation of humans had learned to steal the innocence of very young children and to defy laws that could perhaps destroy a covenant between God and man. The lust directed toward children of God outraged Ozz far beyond his level of tolerance. The archangel Chism, had been appointed to represent his grievance pertaining to the limits of Earth Angels in light of the surge in child rape occurrences.

The following morning, the man on Hamilton Avenue began to contemplate what he was going to do with Sissy. *I can't let her go,* he thought, *she would surely tell someone and I might end up in prison.* He glanced over at the small child who hadn't eaten for at least a day. She was lying helplessly curled up in the corner on the pile of dirty clothes where he had sexually abused her in every way imaginable.

He slowly walked over to the child and for the first time since he had brought her here, he did not become erect. Before this day he had never thought of himself as a rapist, but now suddenly he realized that he was. He had committed the unforgivable act of violating a child. He could feel himself beginning to panic. With each breath he took, fear of what might happen to him increased.

He wondered what evil had caused him to yield to such cruelty and lustfulness. Where had this urge to inflict enough dominance to momentarily make the child sexually and morally his come from? Where did it come from and where had it gone? She was just an ordinary child now. The spontaneous sexual hunger that drove him to violate her had vanished, leaving him with a desire to take his own life.

*Oh, my Lord, what have I done?* he thought, *There might be a better way than killing myself. No one saw me with her. I'll just bury her and no one will ever know.*

The man lifted Sissy up from the rag pile and carried her to the basement where he laid her down on her back and began to cover her with the debris and garbage that was scattered around on the floor. Sissy was awakened by the weight of the garbage that was already covering the lower part of her body. Once more she began to cry. The man looked at her in a sorrowful way, and continued to gather whatever he could find to bury with.

After a few moments, he paused and bent over her. "What do you want me to do little girl?" he sadly asked her. "What do you want me to do?"

Sissy very quickly responded, "Die. I want you to die!"

At the same time, in the place where angels wait, Chism asked Ozz. "What would you like to do? We aren't capable of harming a soul."

"I- I want to kill him! I want that damned man to die for hurting her. I want him to die. Die! Die! Die, you bastard!" he said as he slammed his hand onto the stone table.

"Die," said the five-year-old Sissy. "Die."

The angels were suddenly startled by the loud and eerie moan of a man in pain.

"Oh, my God! Oh-h-h! Oh-h-h!" the man on Hamilton Avenue moaned, the sound echoing through the room. "Oh, my God," the voice moaned again, then grasped chest as his heart began to pour through his fingers. "Oh, my God," he moaned with his eyes now bursting out from their sockets as he fell to his knees in pain.

Little Sissy lifted herself up using every bit of strength she had within her. The man from Hamilton Avenue was now lying on the concrete floor just across the room. He was shaking violently. Sissy ran up the stairs as fast as her small legs would allow. "Die," she whispered, "that's what I want you to do. Die!" She squeezed through the door that was partially blocked by an old refrigerator, and ran out onto the street. *Home,* she thought, *I'm going home.*

She walked for what seemed like hours, until she finally came to her own front yard. Entering through the front door she called out, "Mommy! Mommy!" No one was home. She walked into the kitchen and grabbed an open loaf of bread from the counter top that she could barely reach. She opened the refrigerator and drank directly from a quart of milk until her thirst was under control.

"Mommy?" she called out again as she walked through the house, but got no answer. Exhausted, she climbed onto the couch and fell off to sleep.

# CHAPTER 2

"What have you done, Ozz?" Chism asked as the man's voice ceased. "What have we done?"

"I don't know. I just don't know," Ozz said. "I was so filled rage that I had never felt before. What does this mean? What do you think has happened?"

"Where is Sissy?"

"I don't know. She is not crying out as she was."

"I don't feel her presence. Do you think he has taken her life?" Ozz asked.

"Find her! Seek the presence of her heart; maybe you can save her. Concentrate, you fool, she must be in worse danger than before," Chism demanded.

"I can't feel her. The cries of the man have blocked my senses. Come on," said Ozz.

"Where are we going?"

"We're going to Hamilton Avenue."

As they approached the vacant house they had to walk through a crowd that had gathered to hear why the police and the coroner had roped off the area surrounding a house that no one has lived in for years. Without being seen, the two angels went inside. Still, Ozz could not feel Sissy's presence. They hurried to where she had been, and saw the man who had cried out lying dead on the floor. They listened to the coroner as he summarized what might have happened.

"I've never seen anything like this before," the coroner said. "He seems to have exploded from within, yet he screamed so loud the neighbors three to four houses away heard him. Look, he's holding his own heart in his hand like he ripped it out of his chest in a fit of anger."

"Come on," said Ozz.

"Where are we going now?"

"Sissy has gone home. I can feel her."

Chism and Ozz left the house and headed toward South Street. Ozz looked directly into the small frame house.

"This is it," Ozz said, "She's inside." They rushed up the concrete steps and onto the front porch. Without hesitation they entered. Ahead and to their right was a flight of stairs to the second floor bedrooms. To their left was a doorway leading into the living room.

"This way," said Ozz, pulling Chism into the living room. Though it was daylight, the room was dark because the curtains were closed. Sissy was curled up in a corner of the couch, fast asleep.

"There she is. My God, I'm so glad she's alive," Ozz said. "No, don't touch her, she will awaken," he said as Chism sat near her feet.

They both stood looking down at the child in silence.

"It's not going to get any easier for her is it?" asked Ozz.

"I don't know. She's been through so much. I don't know how much longer she can endure without some kind of intervention from heaven or earth."

The two angels were suddenly interrupted by the sound of footsteps.

"Someone's coming'" said Chism.

Just then, Sissy's mother entered through the front door with Sissy's two older brothers. They came into the living room and spotted Sissy lying on the couch.

"Where have you been? You better not tell me you were at Floyd's all this time," said Sissy's mother in a disciplinary tone, startling Sissy out of her sleep.

"Momma," Sissy said, looking hopeful at being welcomed home.

"Don't momma me. Where have you been?" her mother demanded.

"I was hurt, Momma. A man took me into a old house and hurt me."

"What are you sayin' child? If your tellin' a story I swear I'll tear you up!"

"No, Momma, it's true. He hurt me, and I got away, I swear."

"You ain't talkin' about Floyd?"

"No, Momma."

"Get up. Let's go. We'll see about this," Sissy's mother said while pulling the child toward the door. "You boys stay here 'til I come back," She took Sissy by the hand and left the house, pulling her along. They walked across North Avenue toward Green Street.

"Where did it happen?"

"I don't know, Momma."

"Was it up by where Floyd works?"

"I don't know, Momma. I think so."

"Was it the next street over or further?"

"I think it was the next street. Momma, I don't wanna go back. Please, Momma, I'm scared!"

"We're gonna walk over on Hamilton Avenue. I want you to show me where it happened."

Hazel, Sissy's mother, was a twenty-four year old who didn't smoke or do drugs. She occasionally had a few drinks but seldom to the point of intoxication. Her biggest weakness was her overwhelming and uncontrolled sexual desire. She had an ongoing fear that Henry, her husband, and Floyd, her lover, might stop satisfying her unending sexual appetite.

She was an average looking five foot six inch light complexioned young woman with straight long black hair. Her facial features were attractive but her battle scars from Henry kept her from being called beautiful. She kept her fingernails polished a bright red, which often matching her lipstick. She could easily pass for white when and if it was convenient to do so.

She often moved about nervously as if she were about to run at any moment. She spoke quickly and sometimes stuttered in search of her words. All three of her children were the result of her unrelenting hunger for sex; she'd never wanted children.

She always had that look about her that said, "If a man were to just ask, I'd yield myself without a hint of resistance."

She had been suspicious that Floyd had something to do with Sissy not coming home, yet she didn't call the police. She was afraid of losing her lover and afraid that Henry would use this as another excuse to draw her into another fights. She had no intentions of letting Henry suspect that she had sent Sissy out into the night to service Floyd. Hazel had assured Henry that Sissy was visiting her mother and would be returning shortly.

Actually, Hazel thought it would have been better if Sissy hadn't returned. She did, though, and now she had a problem. Sissy not only came home, she came home and had been raped by someone other than Floyd.

As they turned onto Hamilton, a passing police car noticed Hazel dragging Sissy along behind her. "Is there anything wrong?" the officer asked after stopping and rolling down his window.

Hazel quickly said no and continued dragging Sissy down the sidewalk. She looked surprised when the officer pulled to the curb and asked again, "Are you sure there isn't anything wrong?"

"She said she was raped," Hazel said while pushing Sissy toward the officer.

"What?"

"She said somebody raped her in a old house somewhere up here on Hamilton. Tell 'em, what you told me," she said while gesturing from Sissy to the officer, "Go ahead, tell 'em."

After hearing this, the officer radioed headquarters. "Listen," he said into his microphone, "we have a mother and a small child at the corner of Green Street and North Wood. The mother says the child was raped at an old house on Hamilton. Isn't that where they found the body this morning?"

A voice over the radio responded, "Affirmative. Take them to the house. We'll have the captain there in a few minutes."

When the captain got to the house, he asked Sissy, "What did he look like? Where did it happen? Come and show me where."

Sissy followed the policeman as they entered into the doorway where the boarding had been removed.

"Is this the place?" he asked while pointing into the room where the dead body had been found. "Is this where it happened?"

"Tell the man, Sissy. Is this the place? You know how to talk, girl. You tell the man. Is this it?"

Sissy nodded her head yes. She was confused and frightened. So much had happened in such a short period of time.

"How did you get away?" another officer asked. "How did you get out?"

"Wait. Just wait," the captain said. "You can't be suggesting this child killed that guy. Get serious. Come on, let's get her to Children's Hospital to be checked out. When the coroner files his report we'll know if he committed suicide after the child got away. I'm sorry miss, what is your name?"

"Williams," Sissy's mother said, "My name is Hazel Williams. My daughter's name is Joyce but we call her Sissy."

# CHAPTER 3

"Why do you think she took Sissy from the house in such a rush without calling the police or taking her to the hospital?" Chism asked Ozz.

"I don't know, maybe she wanted to make sure it wasn't Floyd or maybe she thought she knew who it was," replied Ozz.

"There is evil here and it seems to be coming for Sissy. Maybe, God willing, she'll make it out of this hell with her sanity intact. Or maybe, like so many others, she'll give up," said Chism.

"I'm sticking with her. I'm going to do what I can to keep her strong, no matter what it takes or what I have to do," Ozz responded.

"You know in your sector alone we have watched young mothers turn their heads to so many of the evil acts committed against their children. It seems like the majority of the time they play ignorant because of their own selfish desire to maintain what they believe to be love," Chism said.

"Yes, I agree, but how is it that society has come to the point that violent acts against children can be tolerated?" asked Ozz.

"There is obviously a certain similarity in vulnerable females. Consequently, men like Floyd have learned to not only recognize these subliminally projected weaknesses but to create an approach that's difficult for the female to reject."

"What do you mean?" asked Ozz.

"I mean for generations a large number of pedophiles were able to win the trust and unconditional love of the mothers of their targeted victims long before they approached the child. They tend to align themselves with the sexual expectation of the mother. They slowly assure the mother that if such a thing were to occur with a child there is a possibility that it might not be such a bad thing. Once the mother agrees in anyway, they begin to weave their web.

"There are other techniques of course; the most common is to deny any accusation from the child and declare that the child is lying and trying to come between them. There is also the proposition that he or she has been teaching the child in preparation for the sexual experiences to come, although the child may be as young as four or five years of age.

Let me tell you about a young mother in a city nearby that actually made the decision to involve her eight year old daughter in a sexual relationship with an adult for the sake of her own personal satisfaction.

This drug addicted mother of three named Stacy was beginning to lose her high, and Children and Youth Services had previously charged her with neglect because she left her five, seven and eight year olds unattended. She was threatened with jail time if it happened again.

Her phone had been shut off for more than a month, leaving her no way to communicate with her usual drug sources. The empty refrigerator reflected just how desperate she had become. She had sold last month's food stamps for drug money and the children's only available food was cereal until the first of next month.

"Mommy—" one of the children started to speak.

"Shut up and sit down!" she screamed before the child could continue. "Keep your little ass on that couch and don't move until I tell you to. That goes for all of you!" The mother began to panic as the thought of being without drugs set off the alarms in her brain.

There was a small-time drug dealer three houses down the block that sold marijuana but she had long outgrown finding satisfaction in marijuana alone. However, pot would be better than nothing at all and it could probably hold her over until she found a better solution.

"You kids sit right there and don't move. I mean it! Don't even get up. You hear me?" she said while giving the children her customary evil eye.

They all nodded their heads in acknowledgment. Of course the moment the door closed behind her the children were up and actively looking for something to get into.

Stacy made her way over to the home of the small-time drug dealer and knocked on the front door. A short, overweight, dark skinned man opened the door and asked Stacy what she wanted.

"Do you got anything?" she asked.

"What you want?"

"Coke," she answered.

"Hell no! You know I don't fuck wit dat. I got some herb and that's it."

"I need somethin' stronger. Can you get me somethin'?"

"How much money you got?"

"I got some money," she replied, "but I can do somethin' for you that's better than money. I'll lay with you and do anything you want."

"You crazy, don't nobody want no coke fiend."

"I ain't a coke fiend, I just wanna get a little high. I know you can get wit dat."

"No I can't git wit that. No money, no drugs."

"Can you just get me a little somethin' 'til I get my check?"

"No, Stacy, 'cause you don't pay up and you know it. Everybody knows it."

"Yes I will, I swear. I'll swear on my daughter's grave. Fine, I'll get yo money."

"Come back in about an hour and I'll see what I can get. But, I'm tellin' you now, I want my money."

"All right, I heard you. I heard you. You'll get the damn money. Don't worry."

Stacy walked back to her house smoking her last cigarette and falling deeper into a pit of fear than she had ever been before. It wasn't a fear of being mugged, robbed or raped; it was a fear that the drug dealer wouldn't come through for her.

When she got back home she was greeted by the sounds of her children playing and running around the house. As she slammed the door behind her, the eight-year-old quickly sat down after she carelessly knocked over and broke a lamp that had been sitting on the end table.

"Look what you did! Get your ass upstairs and don't even think of comin' down 'til I tell you!"

Stacy thought for a few minutes as she began to pick up the pieces of broken lamp. *Fuck this, I'm sick of these kids.* "Come down here right now!"

Her children slowly came down the stairs, afraid of what their mother might do.

"You two sit on that couch and don't move or you'll get what she's gonna get."

"I'm sorry, Momma," her daughter said as she reached the bottom of the stairs.

"Sorry ain't gettin' it. You just come with me." Stacy took her eight-year-old to the drug dealer's front door. She knocked and waited for him to answer.

"Who is it?" he asked from within.

"It's me, Stacy."

He opened the door and looked at Stacy, then down at the child.

"I'll give you my kid as collateral. You can keep her 'til I bring you the money, but I need the drugs now."

"What the hell am I gonna do with a kid?" the dealer asked.

"Whatever you want. Look how pretty she is. She can do your dishes, clean or whatever." Stacy then leaned over and whispered into his ear. "Maybe you can teach her how to please a man. You know what I mean? She's a virgin but she gotta be taught. That's gotta be worth a lot to a man like you."

The drug dealer was speechless but beginning to become aroused. He pulled his head back from Stacy and locked his stare on the young child.

"Yeah, I guess I'll help you out," he said. The child was standing quietly with her head down. "You can leave her here and I'll watch her for you 'til you bring me my money. Here, this is good shit but it's gonna cost two hundred. I want my money. You hear me?"

"Yeah, I heard you. Just gimme dat shit," she said as she snatched it from his hand. She paused and looked down at her eight-year-old, then took her into her arms and squeezed her tightly.

"I love you, baby. Momma will always be here for you. I just need to take care of somethin' and your helpin' me out. You know momma loves you, don't you? Momma's never gonna leave you. Just do this for me. It'll be all right."

Stacy took her drugs home and quickly found her favorite place — the place where there were no hardships and everything was good. There were no problems, fears or discomforts in this world. It was a place where nothing truly matters and perception stays on the side of utopia.

"You know," said Chism, "Stacy reasoned that her first need is to take care of herself in order to take better care of her children. I can see how difficult life can be without food on the table, without a source of money, children without a father, rent that's always two months behind, a constant flow of monthly eviction and shut-off notices. For her to say that 'everything is going to be all right' is simply a lie. Sometimes humans don't realize that the biggest lies ever told are the ones they tell themselves."

The drug dealer was gradually overcome with lust. Later that evening he gave the child several sleeping pills before having his way with her. He, too, became addicted, not to drugs but to the new found pleasure of young girls. He could now focus his attention on drug addicted mothers who would always be willing to make a trade."

"Are you trying to get me to see your point of view?" asked Ozz.

"No, only to consider it," responded Chism, who, as an archangel, was an Angel of Understanding and Wisdom. He was active between the heavenly place and places where souls dwell. There are angels of much higher authority but none are closer to the part of God's domain that recognizes the spirits of mankind.

An Earth angel, such as Ozz, is an Angel of Compassion. It was difficult for the two to understand each other's points of view.

# CHAPTER 4

Two days later, Sissy sat staring at the floor with her feet tucked under her body. So much had happened to her. Her father, Henry Williams, paused in front of her with his head tilted to one side, just enough to catch her eye.

"Are you all right?" he asked.

She didn't answer. She just continued to stare at the floor like she didn't hear him.

"What are you thinkin' about?" he asked in a kind and unusually fatherly voice.

She looked at him without responding and then looked back down towards the floor.

"I know. I know what you're thinkin'," he said. "It'll be all right."

Little Sissy thought those were the kindest words she had ever heard from her father. *Maybe, just maybe he does care about me, though I don't think so. I don't think anyone does. No, no one cares about me. I'm just Sissy, not anybody who counts...*

Henry Williams had been 57 years old at her birth and was now 63. Sissy was his third child. He'd begun dating her mother when she was just twelve years old. At that time, he was 49. Their first child was born when his wife was just 14 years old. Since that time, he subjected Sissy's mother to a weekly ritual of wife abuse.

Often, Sissy had to witness her mother and father physically fighting. Once it even came to the point of her father drawing his knife and threatening to kill her mother. After that, Sissy stayed to herself, not speaking a single word for days to avoid drawing any attention to herself.

Many times, after fighting with her mother, her father came into her bedroom and climbed into bed with her. *My daddy,* she thought during those times, *he loves me. I can trust him and know that he wouldn't do anything to hurt me. If daddy does it, it must be all right. It must be what is supposed to happen. He's so big and strong; he could crush anything or anybody who might try to hurt me. I can always trust my daddy.*

At age five, Sissy had no idea that what her father was doing wasn't a normal occurrence. Many times he laid his head upon her small shoulders and whispered loving words as if she was a grown woman. Many times he kissed her passionately. Other times he put his hands on her body like she was a grown woman. So many of those times he hurt her beyond belief with his words of love and affection.

*He was so much kinder than Floyd. Floyd is mean; my daddy treated me like I was his special baby. Floyd hurt me over and over again with laughter in his voice. I don't know, maybe it's just me. At least no one else gets hurt. I'm always the one who gets hurt.*

She began to realize that her father would be heading off to work soon and worried she might be in store for another miserable night. *Everyone else will be able to sleep and look forward to tomorrow, while I lie here and hope someone will take me away to a happy place so I don't have to live through another tomorrow like today.*

# CHAPTER 5

"Who in their right mind would put their own five year old in danger by sending her out to a warehouse at night with a meal for the likes of Floyd?" asked Ozz.

"No, no one in their right mind. We're not talking about anyone who is in their right mind; we're talking about a mother who has been sexually and physically abused for more years than Sissy. She has no right mind. An inhuman disease that has been blinding to an astonishing number of mothers has infected her. She has totally given up on the possibility of protecting her daughter. She uses all her energies to protect herself," Chism said.

"That's ridiculous, we're talking about her baby. She should be willing and ready to die for the safety and happiness of her child."

"Normally that's true, but think about it. She's been a part of the sexual abuse. Her parents gave her into a relationship with a 49-year-old demented abuser. She thought it might be the right thing. She believed that it must be a common act in families. As twisted as it sounds, she has probably convinced herself that it's not so bad to be a sex object for those who claim they love you. She, too, was a victim," said Chism.

"Yes, she was. But, now she is not the victim anymore. She is just as guilty as her sick lovers. She's aware of their abuses and does nothing to stop them. She is a coward who has accepted that it is better for her five-year-old to go through it like she did, than for her to disrupt her relationship with Floyd interrupt the sick pleasures her husband once found in her as a child.

She is despicable and warrants the same kind of death as the man on Hamilton," said Ozz.

"Watch what you say. Remember that we may be partially responsible for that gruesome death. That is not our purpose. We both know that we may have overstepped our boundaries.

"You and I, and others like us, have stood by when we were aware of these demented acts being forced upon children. We did this without stepping up and stopping them just as her mother idly watches her child being defiled. Maybe we're as bad as she is." asked Ozz said.

"Yes, but we cannot intervene. We are not earth's children. We are closer to God. There are boundaries that we cannot violate."

"What I know is that between my wish for the destruction of that man on Hamilton and little Sissy's wish for his death, somehow we caused his demise. I wonder if I am becoming as men. I wonder if I have found a way to punish those who I have learned to despise," stated Ozz.

"I cannot answer that question for you. I have no right to judge or to take a life; but I must admit to you and I'm sure God knows as well, I found satisfaction and pleasure in the death of that child rapist," Chism said.

Ozz was experiencing a new emotion that sewn a new piece of character into his being. He decided he would refuse to just watch as bad things happened. He knew that he and his comrade would again feel the need to sneak across the line and punish the evil. So far there has been no repercussion from the death of the man on Hamilton. Maybe, just maybe, they had stumbled upon a permissible act of retaliation.

# CHAPTER 6

*One year later...*

Sissy sat in her first grade classroom. She wondered why all the other kids seemed so joyful and happy. They always looked forward to playing and going home at the end of the school day. She didn't have the same anticipation for playtime and she certainly didn't look forward to going home. Despite everything that had happened to her, her grades were far above average and she found that all her lessons were easy.

She gazed out the window of Franklin Elementary School and thought about the upcoming Christmas holiday. She remembered when she'd overheard one of the kids next door talking about Santa and what it takes to get the toys that you want on Christmas morning. The neighborhood children got gifts every year. Sissy searched for a reason why Santa rejected her. The other kids told her it might be because she'd been bad or maybe she hadn't listened to her parents. But she did listen and she tried to do everything they asked.

Last Christmas Eve, she'd left out milk and cookies just like the little girl next door said to do. The only thing she hadn't done was write a letter telling Santa what she wanted. *Maybe that was why he didn't come,* she thought.

This year she was going to write one, and hoped that was the missing piece that would solve the mystery of why Santa never visited her.

Shortly before Christmas she wrote to Santa and she personally put the letter into the mailbox. It read:

*Dear Santa Claus,*

*I hope you will have a present for me this year. I have been a good girl this time, and nobody is mad at me. I wish for a Barbie doll with clothes. Please try to bring me one. I will leave you some cookies and milk like Sally did.*

*P.S. I hope you don't pass me by this year.*

*Sissy*


Sissy couldn't wait. Christmas, according to what they said on television, was only three shopping days away. Two of the days passed quickly. Now with just one day left, her level of excitement was at its peak.

Unfortunately, Henry and Floyd's level of excitement was also high, and they both took advantage of Sissy's desire to be good for Christmas. On Christmas Eve each of the predators visited little Sissy's bedroom long before Santa was to arrive. Sissy stayed focused. She had no intention of letting her father or Floyd dash her hopes of getting a Barbie doll.

Early Christmas morning, around 7 a.m., Sissy sprang up from her bed like millions of other children her age. Unlike those children, though, Sissy's home had no decorations Christmas tree. In fact, there was no special place to look for a gift from Santa, so she'd created her own.

The house was silent and no one else was awake. Sissy quietly and slowly made her way to the bottom of the stairwell, peaking around each corner to be sure that Santa was gone, because she'd heard that you were never supposed to see him. Since there was no Christmas tree, she knew to head for her hiding place in the living room where she'd left the cookies and milk.

After carefully looking around the room, she walked over to the far end of the couch and nervously got down onto her hands and knees. With excitement bubbling up inside her, she tilted her head and leaned down enough to see behind the couch. The cookies and milk she'd left for Santa were still there, undisturbed. Her heart sank and she leaned back against the side of the couch. She put her thumb into her mouth and began to rock back and forth. She tried not to cry with all her might.

"It's all right," she assured herself. "Maybe he'll come tomorrow." That day, she watched as the children next door played with all the toys Santa had left for them. Somehow, she knew that her wish was not going to come true. *For some reason, Santa must have decided I didn't deserve a gift. I'll just have to try harder.* She was determined to be the best little girl in the entire world. She wasn't going to give up, not ever.

Christmas had never been a happy time in her house. As far back as she could remember, her parents used the occasion to invite adult friends over as a prelude of one of their holiday sparring matches. The fights always ended with her being subjected to her father's sick sexual appetite or Floyd celebrating his manhood by inflicting as much fear and pain on her as he could.

Every time this happened, and it wasn't always at Christmas time, she wondered, *Why why me? Why doesn't someone do something to stop them? Why doesn't mommy make them stop? Does everyone else go through this too?*

She just assumed this was the way things had to be. She eventually gave up hoping things would change. After all, what was happening to her has been happening for as long as she could remember. She found no reason to think they'd stop. *Maybe this is normal,* she thought. *It's odd, though, that they don't do this with my brothers. I guess I'm special, but I really don't want to be special in that way.*

# CHAPTER 7

Sissy recalled a short time ago she and her siblings were watching television one Saturday afternoon, while her mother grudgingly washed clothes in the basement. The back door opened and then slammed shut. Their daddy had gone out no more than ten minutes before. They knew who it was.

Like so many times before, the two older boys would made their escape out the front door and headed out onto the streets — it was safer there. Floyd seemed to know not to bother them, anyway. Sissy listened as he rummaged through the kitchen, calling out her mother's name.

"Hazel?" he yelled, "God-damn-it! Hazel, you hear me? I ain't got but a minute and I need somethin' to eat!" Hazel couldn't hear him in the basement, and continued washing clothes. "Hazel!" he yelled at the top of his lungs.

Sissy heard the refrigerator door slam and knew he was headed her way. "Oh please! Oh please," she quietly prayed, "let him not notice me." She put her head down and closed her eyes hoping he wouldn't notice her. She listened as he quickly came closer to the living room. She squeezed her eyes closed tighter as she felt him getting closer.

"Please," she whispered, "don't let him see me."

Her body tensed. She thought that the closing of her eyes would help take her from his view. She remained that way as long as she could. She heard the cartoons playing on the television, but no other sound. She thought maybe he'd gone away. She began to release the tension in her body and opened one eye long enough to see if he had passed through the room.

Floyd patiently stood above her with an ugly grin on his face, waiting for her to open her eyes. When she saw him standing over her she began kicking and screaming as loud as she could, accidentally kicking Floyd in his groin. That sent him to his knees in pain, but he recovered quickly. He stood up and looked at her with anger.

"Please stop!" Sissy screamed.

He grabbed Sissy by both of her ankles and jerked her into the air, causing her to dangle while he struck her as hard as he could on her rear end.

"You little bitch!" he yelled. "If I had time, I'd take you up stairs and teach you the lesson of your life." He struck her again and threw her small body onto the sofa.

Sissy continued to scream, "I hate you! I hate you!"

"You wait and see what I do to you tonight, you little brat."

"I'm going to tell my daddy! He'll get you," Sissy screamed.

"Your daddy? Go ahead and tell your daddy, he ain't gonna do nothin' but finish what I started on your little butt."

By now Sissy's mother had come upstairs to see what all the noise was about.

"You better get that little brat, she kicked me in my balls," he said.

"Did you Sissy? What do you think your doin'?"

"He hit me! I hate him, Mommy! I hate him!"

"You shut up right now," said her mother.

"I'm going to tell my daddy," Sissy repeated.

"No you're not. Get upstairs right now. I'll deal with you later," Hazel said menacingly.

Floyd rolled his eyes and grinned at Sissy as she got up and headed up the stairs.

"Yeah," he said, "I'll take care of you tonight."

When she got upstairs, Sissy climbed onto her bed and settled back into her calm and passive personality. She didn't know what had gotten into her.

She realized that she was going to be in trouble the moment Floyd found her alone.

As the night came on, she lay alone and scared, and every sound caused her to become rigid with fear. She lay awake as hour after hour passed. She hoped that the first voice she heard would be her father's.

In the wee hours of the morning Sissy was awakened by the sound she dreaded. Someone was downstairs. *Who is it, daddy or Floyd?* She could hear footsteps as whoever they were walked through the downstairs hall and started up the steps. She covered her head with her pillow and curled into the fetal position.

The person reached the top of the stairs and stopped for what seemed like forever. "Please don't come in here," she whispered.

She listened but couldn't hear anything. *He must still be standing in the hall,* she thought. She pulled the pillow off her head, and she could hear breathing but she still couldn't figure out who it was. She heard the hall light click on and the light reflected onto the wall beside her bed. She wanted to look but she was afraid.

She began to whimper uncontrollably, but not loud enough that she could not be heard. She curled her body up tighter and put her thumb in her mouth. She knew she couldn't run or call out without causing more trouble for herself.

She was trying to remain as still as she could with her eyes shut tightly until who ever it was went away. The floorboards squeaked as someone walked softly towards her in an attempt not to be heard. Again, she heard breathing. This time the breathing was closer than before. She knew who it was. She could smell the stink coming off his body.

She slightly uncovered her head to see where he was. She heard the rustling of his clothes as they were being undone. As his clothes hit the floor at her bedside she squirmed and curled up even tighter. The bed sank deeply behind her as the weight of his body pulled her toward him. He lifted the covers behind her and then he spoke.

"Ah-ha," he said. "What do we have here? A nice little present for Floyd from yo momma? Now, Floyd's gonna take care of daddy's little girl."

*The Rape Nest*

Sissy remained frozen. She could feel and smell his breath against the back of her neck as he grabbed one of her fee. She suddenly screamed and yanked her foot out of his grasp while managing to get out of her bed. Floyd tangled himself in the bed covers and couldn't grab her as she moved as fast as she could out of the room.

"Momma! Momma!" she yelled, as she made it into the hall and pushed her mother's bedroom door open. As the hall light lit her mother's bedroom, she looked into her open eyes.

"Momma, tell him to leave me alone!" By now Floyd had caught up with her.

"Momma!" Sissy repeated in a pleading child's voice. "Tell him to leave me alone. Please, Momma." Her mother looked directly into her eyes and started to speak, but stopped. She then quietly rolled over with her back to Sissy. Floyd lifted Sissy off the floor and carried her back to her bed.

As always, Ozz watched and listened in anger that words could not describe.

# CHAPTER 8

"It stands to reason," said Ozz to Chism, "that if we were the cause of the death of the child rapist on Hamilton we must have some level of ability to intervene with a person who commits an evil act against a child."

"But God has not given us that right," responded Chism. "We have somehow stumbled upon the possibility that we can avenge the innocent by simply wishing it so."

"I don't want to sit idly by while these sick men take away the innocence of these small children. What are we if we don't try to stop them?"

"We are angels. We don't kill without God's authority. We are here to soothe the souls and spirits of humans, not the mind and body. We are messengers of God."

"Why can't we try?" asked Ozz. "If we are capable of anger to the degree of hate, why can't we try?"

"Because we do not hate mankind, we hate the actions of sin, we hate acts of ignorance. We sometimes hate coincidental tragedy, but we are not supposed to be capable of hating human beings," Chism responded.

"But we do! Not only have we hated, we have also wished for the deaths of those who ruthlessly harm those with innocent hearts," said Ozz.

"But we should not. Evil has a way of entering into the minds and bodies of not only the weak-minded, but also the strong-minded. Hate and evil can infect a good man as well. We must adhere to God's word. These humans are to be forgiven with the acceptance of His existence," Chism said.

"No!" said Ozz, "I can no longer stand by and watch. We have lost our value. We cannot possibly soothe the soul of a mother who has lost her son or daughter to a human who has found himself arrogant and proud enough to disregard the pleas of a helpless child. To violently rape and torture a child to satisfy his or her lust for dominance should not be forgiven with a mere prayer. So many souls cry out for the removal of evil before it moves on to its next victim. Let's defy God and go to the aide of the helpless children. Come on, Chism. Please be with me. We are not just messengers, we could also be peacekeepers," Ozz pleaded.

"These abuses are so widespread that we would never rest. Listen. Even as we speak there are thousands of children crying out."

"That is why you and I should work to rid the world of this disease for the sake of those children. We can start with Sissy who has been raped and mistreated by her own father and her father's friend while her mother stands idly by and pretends she doesn't see. We are no better than she is now that we know we can intervene, but don't," Ozz said passionately.

"I want to act. I want to say to children like Sissy, 'We are here for you. God has sent us.' I want to strike down the man who has found his own safety by instilling fear. I want vengeance for the innocent we are here to watch over. I want this type of predator to feel God's vengeance before the devil leaves his body, before he completes his feeling of pleasure."

Ozz paused and looked directly into Chism's eyes when he did not respond and was deep into thought.

*Ozz might be right in the way he feels about vengeance,* Chism thought. *I, too, feel the need to strike down the grinning faces of the likes of Floyd.* Chism had also felt pleasure when that rapist and a would-be murderer burst from within. *After all, why shouldn't we be able to answer the pleas of a child? Why is it that an evil man's prayer can be heard and not the child's after he has stepped across the boundary of reason with an offence worse than sin? Thou shalt not rape and murder innocent children and if thou do, thou will suffer the fair and just retaliation of his or her guardian angel.*

"I would love to answer the pleas of the children," Chism finally said. "However, we must remain obedient to God not our own wishes. Think of the possible consequences of our interference."

"Then, I shall ask for forgiveness just as they do and may God have mercy on me, much more mercy than these demented men and women have had on the helpless children they abuse each night. Many humans feel that a sin is a sin. It seems mindless to think that there are similar character traits in a person that steals a loaf of bread and a person who rapes and murders a four-year-old child. Theft can be a lightly punished matter, cold calculated murder cannot. Punishment should fit the crime. We are taking it upon ourselves to take away the lives of those who prey on the helpless, those who are cowards among men and those who are filled with evil.

"But, what if evil abandons their souls and enters another's at death? What if a human body has become a temporary dwelling place for evil beyond the control of the man? Should we still kill the body or should it be spared when the beast abandons it?" asked Chism.

"Is there such a thing as Satan?" Ozz asked. Are there really demons or a beast that enters the minds and souls of men, or is the beast inside the man at the start of his life? Does it just lie in wait for an opportunity to destroy another being's joy of living? The only beasts that Sissy need fear are just simply men who have taken it upon themselves to believe that no one else's peace-of-mind matters. Since the beginning of time, mankind has managed to blame his own evil on the many so-called boogiemen that you and I know do not exist. They all have the common cry of 'the devil made me do it' or 'I was possessed' or 'I must have been temporarily insane' when it is he and only he who is the violator.

"Like you, I feel the desire to eliminate the excuses along with the man," Chism said, "but I feel we must always weigh each matter separately."

"I want to let it be known that we are not only watching, we are willing to defy the rules of heaven and strike a blow for the helpless by removing evil souls from existence. Maybe you and I can start a new way of protection here on earth. One that makes it clear that those who harm a child, can't be saved from our retaliation.

"Let's make a pact," Ozz continued. "Let's sign our covenant with the blood of innocent children. Let it be known that neither God nor heaven nor hope of forgiveness will protect he who has filled himself with enough evil to destroy the hope innocent children. Let's make the pact, Chism. Let's go to their aid in every way and use every weapon we possess as angels."

Chism had not yet responded, but Ozz embraced him like he had agreed.

PART TWO

# HE PLAYED NICK-NACK ON HER KNEE

# CHAPTER 9

Sissy sat alone on the front porch of her home on South Street. She was patiently waiting to start what was to be a very special day. This was the day that one of her older brothers was moving into middle school. There was to be an acceptance and welcome extended to the students and their parents. When her mom finally came out onto the porch with her older children, Sissy gave them one of her rarely seen smiles.

"Sit right there, Sissy. Momma's gonna take your picture," her mother said while attempting to adjust the camera. "Show your pretty little legs, pull up your pant legs for Momma," she said while snapping a couple of shots. "Baby, you stay here with your daddy. Okay? Daddy don't want to be here by himself."

"No, Momma," Sissy pleaded, "I want to go. I never get to go."

"You heard me. Now get in there and keep your daddy company. I'll bring you something back."

"Please, Momma. Why can't I go?" cried Sissy.

"You heard me. Don't make me have to tell you again. I'll bring you back some candy," her mother said.

Sissy ran into the house, angry and disappointed. She parted the front curtains and sadly watched as the rest of the family walked toward the school. She wasn't crying, even though she was really said. This was a common type of letdown for her, and not nearly as bad as others she'd endured.

She continued to watch as the family disappeared from view, hoping that her momma would have a change of heart and call for her to join them.

When that didn't happen, she thought, *Well, at least everyone else got to go. It's usually me who has to miss out on the fun. I wish I could be like them.* Sissy moved away from the window and let the curtain fall closed.

"Come on, baby," her father said in his sweet daddy voice. "Lets go upstairs and lay down until they get back."

"No, Daddy. I'm not sleepy, I just want to play."

"Come on now, baby. Daddy wants his baby to lay on his chest. You can play later," her father pleaded.

"No, Daddy," little Sissy repeated. "I don't want to lie down."

"Get upstairs! Don't argue with me. You're gonna hurt daddy's feelings. I wanna hug my little girl. Come on, let's go," he said in a stronger and more demanding voice. "That's my girl. I love my baby girl," he said while following her up the stairs. "I just love my baby girl."

Once they reached Sissy's bed, Henry decided to try and cheer Sissy up. "Do you remember the nursery rhyme we used to sing together?" he asked.

Sissy shook her head no in response.

"No?" he asked, "Come on, you remember don't you? It went like this: This ole man he played one, he played nick-nack with his thumb," Henry sang as he brushed his thumb between the Sissy's legs, "With a nick-nack, patty wack, give your dad a bone. This ole man came rollin' home." With the word home, he pushed his thumb back between her legs and moved it side to side, tickling her. "That used to make you laugh. You remember, baby?"

Sissy sadly shook her head no again.

"Come on now, I know you remember. Lemme think. How'd it go? Oh, yeah, I remember," he continued. "This ole man, he played two. He played nick-nack on her shoe, with a nick-nack, patty wack, give the dad a bone. This ole man came rollin' home." Again he ended with his thumb between her legs.

Sissy still did not respond, so he continued. "This ole man, he played three, he played nick-nack on her knee." Then he placed both of his hands on her knees and attempted to pull her legs open, "With a nick-nack, patty wack, give the dad a bone. This ole man came rollin' home.

"This ole man played four, he played nick-nack at her door." This time he took his forefinger and poked it between her legs. "With a nick-nack, patty wack, give your dad a bone. This ole man came rollin' home.

"This ole man played five… This is my favorite part! He played nick-nack on her thigh." He paused for a second and put his head down close to her legs and ran his tongue along her thighs. He briefly lifted his head and asked, "You remember that, don't you baby?"

Sissy continued her far away stare, and shook her head no.

Henry stood up and undid his trousers while he continued to sing. "This ole man, he played six, he played nick-nack with his stick. You remember daddy's stick, don't you, baby? I know you remember that," asked encouragingly.

"You remember this stick, don't you?" he said as he held his penis in his hand. "Then it went like this," he said as he pushed Sissy down onto her back. "This ole man, he played seven, he played nick-nack in her heaven." Henry then got on top of her and penetrated her.

"This ole man is comin' home. Let Daddy come home, baby. Come on, let daddy come all the way home," he said as he pulled the child's knees apart farther. "That's my girl. You remember, don't cha, baby," he whispered.

Sissy lay still and as limp as she could. She wondered if her brother was having fun at the new school. He was so excited to be moving up to a higher grade. She couldn't wait for it to be her turn.

Henry was nearing the completion of his act. Sissy knew this by the sounds of her father's pleasure. "Ohh yea, ohhh baby."

# CHAPTER 10

In nearby Arlington, a twenty-three year old stepfather was punishing a four-year-old boy for wetting himself. The form of punishment, while the child's mother was at work, was a cigarette. He used the cigarette to burn the child's back and buttocks. The child had endured so much pain that he had passed out while the man continued to find pleasure in inflicting pain.

Simultaneously, in nearby Chevy Chase, while a mother was asleep, a young stepfather attempted to stop his two-year-old daughter from crying.

"Shut up, child! Shut up!" he shouted as he spanked her on her bare bottom as hard as he could.

The child continued to cry louder.

"Shut the hell up, you little bitch!" he screamed at the top of his lungs. He took off his belt and struck the child four or five times with a vengeance. The mother continued to sleep through the crying and screaming.

The stepfather wasn't done. The two-year-old, after continuously being beaten, wet herself. When he witnessed the urine streaming down her legs, he struck her as hard as he could time and time again before realizing that her legs had welts and were bleeding.

The mother, who was in an adjacent room, was still asleep. He went into the bathroom and began filling the tub with hot water, while the two-year-old still continued to scream at the top of her lungs. In complete anger he yanked the child up by her wrist and carried her at arms length into the bathroom where he dropped her into the tub of scalding hot water. The child splashed for a few seconds and then went into shock. She was dead within minutes.

"I knew that would shut you up," he said, as he watched her take her last breath. Her mother, again, was still asleep.

Little Sissy was laying nude on her father's bare chest with tears steaming down the side of her face.

"I love my little Sissy," he mumbled, as he lifted himself up and walked away from his child.

Sissy got up and wandered over to the window. She had lain with her father for what seemed like hours and yet it was still daylight outside. She looked up and down the street, hoping to see her family on their way home.

***

"These are candidates," said Ozz, after witnessing these scenes, "It's time for us to act. I can no longer stand by and watch."

Ozz had balled up both fists in anger. He once again pounded on the stone table where they often stood. "Burn!" he said, directed at the man using his cigarette to torture his son. "Burn! Burn! Burn!" he shouted.

"May your heart burst within your chest!" he shouted, at the man who had drowned his two-year-old daughter. "Slowly," he added.

"I want you to swell slowly until you burst like an over filled trash bag. For you, the special father, the rapist of infants," Ozz said to Sissy's father. "May the air you breathe turn to sand and choke off your deceptive life."

Just as quickly as his rage had flared, it subsided.

The angels sat on the floor at the base of the very table Ozz had been pounding upon. The few moments of hatred depleted him of all of his strength. They sat facing each other wondering what had just happened.

"What have we done?" asked Chism. "Should we have projected forgiveness instead of hate?"

"We showed more mercy than any of the three men we've cursed," answered Ozz. "Let the children forgive them or leave it to God Himself."

***

Back in Arlington, after burning the child with his cigarette until he became tired, the stepfather went into the kitchen. He slammed a pot onto the stove and turned on the gas. "Damn it," he said, "this stupid stove is driving me crazy."

He went back into the living room where the tortured child lay unconscious on the floor. He kicked the small child and picked up the cigarette lighter off the end table and returned to the kitchen.

He flicked the lighter and ignited the gas. The propane and natural gas flashed. In an instant the man's shirtsleeve burst into flames. He tried to douse the flames at the sink, but it didn't work. The propane had saturated his clothing. He pulled and tore off pieces of his burning clothing before the fast-spreading flames overcame him. After a few moments, he was totally engulfed. Later, the small tortured boy walked into the kitchen and found his stepfather lying on the floor, burned beyond recognition.

Over in Chevy Chase, after the man held his child under scalding hot water to keep her from crying, he realized she had breathed her last breath.

"Oh, my God!" he cried, "I didn't mean to hurt you! Honey? Honey!" he shouted to his wife, "There's something wrong with the baby! Honey, hurry!"

He suddenly realized that his wife had slept through the whole incident and perhaps he could take the child's body and dispose of it and place the blame on someone else. He didn't care who was blamed, as long as it wasn't him. He hurriedly lifted her body from the tub and carried her out the back door. He put her into the trunk of his car, then got in and drove towards Washington by way of the beltway. He turned onto Route 295 heading into Anacostia Park and along the river. He found a secluded turn-off that led down to the riverbank.

By now it had gotten dark. He backed his car as close as he could to the rushing water and jumped out to open the trunk. "I'm not close enough," he said to himself.

He got back into his car and backed a little closer to the water. He put the car in park and started to remove the key. *Too close!* he thought to himself. *I'm too close.* He started the car again and slammed it into drive, but the car

*The Rape Nest*

continued to drift backwards. He stomped on the gas pedal trying to drive forward.

"I've got to get out!" he yelled. By now the rear of the car began to float. "I've got to get out!" he said again in a panic, as he opened the door. The current suddenly swept the door completely open.

"Jump! Jump you fool!" yelled at himself.

He jumped out as the car surged towards him and rolled over on its side. In an instant he was pinned beneath the car *with his face buried in the sand.*

*I'm okay,* he thought. *I'm okay. I just need to get my leg free.* He began to spit as his nose and mouth kept filling with sand. *I can't breath! If I could just free my leg, I'll be all right. I've got to keep my head up.*

The car began to slowly sink deeper and deeper. The child abuser sank right along with the car. The body of his victim was still locked in the trunk.

\*\*\*

After satisfying his sexual appetite with his own daughter, as he had done so many times before, a sudden jolt of pain struck in his chest the abuser's chest.

"Sissy?'" he called out. "Sissy, come to Daddy, baby." Again the pain struck, as if someone had stomped on his heart. "Sissy, baby. Come here. Hurry-up, baby."

Sissy came to her father side and stopped just out of his reach.

"Daddy's hurting, baby. I need somebody to help me," he said.

A third jolt caused him to cry out. "Ohhhh, my God! Get on the phone, baby. Call me an ambulance. Hurry, baby, hurry!"

Little Sissy calmly reached out and touched her father's shoulder. "I'll help you, Daddy," she said. Sissy hugged her father around his neck. He was now feeling faint and too weak to speak.

"It's okay," she said. "I won't let them hurt you."

He took a deep breath and released it as all of the pain suddenly left his body. He opened his eyes and found little Sissy now standing above him stroking his eyebrow with her little fingers. "See," she said, "You're all right. They can't hurt you now."

# CHAPTER 11

From out of nowhere the two angels heard Sissy's voice. "No!" They looked at each other, puzzled. "Do you sense Sissy?" Ozz asked.

"Yes, I do, but I don't understand. She seems to be scolding us," replied Chism.

"No!" Sissy said again, more firmly.

"Let's go there. Something strange has happened," said Ozz.

The two angels reached the top steps at Sissy's house and turned to go into her room. There, they found Henry naked and passed out on the bed with Sissy standing over him.

"See?" she repeated. "They can't hurt you."

"Why isn't he dead?" asked Ozz.

"I don't know. Maybe we can't harm humans after all. Apparently we were wrong," Chism said.

"But I felt it in my heart," said Ozz. "I felt him give in to death. Look, Chism, she seems to be looking right at us."

"She can't possibly see us. Humans can't see us. But you're right, it does seem like she's looking right at us," said Chism.

"Don't hurt my daddy," Sissy said while looking directly at the two angels. Ozz and Chism were stunned.

"She's talking to us. That's impossible. She can't talk to us," said Ozz.

"She is. She's talking to us," Chism replied.

"Why do you want to hurt my daddy?" Sissy asked.

Again the angels looked at each other without responding.

"Who is she talking to?" asked Chism.

"Why don't you have wings?" Sissy asked.

Ozz shook his head. "This can't be."

The angel's thoughts were interrupted by the voice of Sissy's mother who had just come through the front door. "Where are you, Sissy?" she called out.

"Up here, Momma! I'm up here! Daddy's sick!"

Her mother rushed up the steps and to his bedside. "Henry?" she said, "Are you okay? What's wrong?"

Henry opened his eyes slightly and said, "I had a dream, I think. I had a pain in my heart like it was going to explode. I dreamed I was about to die and then someone touched me and ... and then everything was all right."

"Well, you must've screamed in your sleep because Sissy was talkin' about you being sick. She needs to go to bed," her mother said.

# CHAPTER 12

"Let's find the other two men we cursed and see if we had any affect on either of them," Ozz said to Chism.

They headed for the home of the torched child in Arlington first. When they arrived, the man lay dead on the kitchen floor with the child looking on in a trance-like state.

On they went to the Chevy Chase site, where they knew the two-year-old had been drowned. They saw the father putting the child's body into the trunk of his car.

"We've failed to protect any of them. We are no better than the humans who stand together and chant silly words in an effort to reach the dead. We have attempted to bring the living to their well-deserved deaths, and just like the chanters, we have failed," said Chism.

"How is it that it worked to destroy the rapist on Hamilton Street and nowhere else? How is it that Sissy was able to protect her father? We'll have to try harder," said Ozz.

"Yes, we will," Chism responded.

The two angels didn't know that two of the three men they had rightfully chosen to destroy would meet death, nor did they realize that Sissy's love for her father was stronger than her ability to hate. She did not want him to die or to be harmed; she only wished that he wouldn't touch her. Her love had saved him from their wrath.

# CHAPTER 13

Floyd started this Sunday just as he had every other one for the last four years — thinking about Sissy and talking to Hazel. "How's Henry?"

"They're going to keep him for a couple of days for some kind of observation. That means you can stay with me tonight and tomorrow," she answered.

"What hospital's he in?" asked Floyd.

"He's over at Mercy. Why? You goin' over to see him?" she joked.

"Naw, I'm just gonna take care of his wife and kid while he's gone." Floyd smiled and rubbed his hands together as he contemplated the fun he was going to have.

"I think we should go over to da church. The bishop say he wants to see us come more often. You and Henry need to start goin', and me to, I guess."

"I ain't been there on a Sunday in years," said Hazel.

"We meet with da bishop first Monday of every month. I don't need to go on no Sunday to hear dem folks screamin' and hollerin'. When we meet da bishop, we don't talk 'bout Christian stuff, we talk 'bout virgins. You know that. I ain't got to tell you. Da bishop just loves those pretty young girls helpin' him with the blessin'." Floyd laughed and slapped his knee in self-approval.

Sissy was sound asleep and deep into a reoccurring dream. She dreamed that her two brothers were reaching out to her as she stood facing the two of them. Instead of embracing her they both began to reach inside of her through her chest and down into her stomach and then began to push against the inside of her private parts. Sissy was frightened and began to wake up. When she woke, she realized that Floyd had come into her room in the middle of the night and was having his way with her just as he had with her mother earlier that night. Again Sissy's soul cried out.

"Please, hear my plea," the young child continued to cry as he ruthlessly continued to grin and make his grunting noises. Sissy gave up her pleas when he left and went back to sleep.

Chism and Ozz, hearing her, again came to her aid. Up the familiar staircase they rushed to find Hazel standing at the open door watching Floyd molest her daughter. She had one of her hands fondling between her own legs and the other was at her breast. She leaned back against the door frame while keeping the sight of Sissy and Floyd in full view.

"My God," said Ozz, "look at her! She knows! That sick woman is using her own daughter to enhance her demented sexual pleasure. Let's kill both of them. Let's strike them down without pity!"

"How?" asked Chism. "How can we strike them down? We've tried, but it didn't work. It is like we are being tortured, too. We are made to know and see evil at its worst and can do nothing about it. He laughs because she is a child of God. What greater pleasure can evil have than to inflict pain and indignity on the innocent? Look at him. He's proud of his hateful dominance. He feels the power of dominating the good. What can we do? Killing him is not enough. The likes of Floyd and the evil in him cannot be harmed. He's protected by God's decision. We've got to find our way to the roots of evil and pull it out like a rotten vine," said Chism.

"Well, they've won this time, but we will have the last laugh," vowed Ozz. "We will find this root of evil and squeeze it until the likes of Floyd have gone to answer to God, and may God have no mercy on them!"

As Chism and Ozz turned to leave, they peered back at Sissy. "She must be strong until we can comfort her and bring her peace," said Ozz.

A loud, spine-chilling laugh that only the two angels could hear sounded from out of nowhere. Both Floyd and Hazel were still deep into their acts of perversion. Again the laugh sounded and shook the loose glass in the window seals. Chism and Ozz felt the ice of fear for the first time. As both Floyd and Hazel reached the climatic end of their pleasure, the laughter sounded a third and final time.

The fear had briefly instilled the two angels with power. As they both headed for the child, they somehow managed to throw Floyd off the bed onto the floor. With all the might the two angels could muster, they formed a protective aura around Sissy.

Hazel didn't feel the presence of the angels or hear the loud laughing voice, but she did see Floyd being thrown to the floor. They both quickly scurried back to the master bedroom.

Ozz strained as he and Chism put off a glow of golden light around the child.

"Hold on Chism," said Ozz, "Hold on a little longer. There's something or someone here that needs to know Sissy's not alone." The two angels held their glow until they felt the evil force subside.

When they were assured that Sissy was safe for the time being, they got up and headed to the heavens to prepare for a battle they didn't feel prepared to fight.

As they disappeared, they heard the whispering voice of the child say, "Thank you."

# CHAPTER 14

When Chism and Ozz returned to their safe haven, they were greeted by three of the senior angels who had been sent by a higher spiritual force. The momentary fear Chism and Ozz experienced had triggered the concerns of the Archangels. The angels wanted two questions answered. The first was, what caused their encounter with such an evil presence on Hill Avenue? The second, why had they taken it upon themselves to break the rules of God and attempt to take a human life?

"What happened here?" asked one of the senior angels. "Who gave you and Chism the right to interfere with the humans?"

"We stand humbly before you, sir," Ozz said. "We have tendered love and affection to all beings. When children are mistreated, we have been there to help them forgive, forget and heal. We have watched as thousands of children met their deaths at the hands of evil and intentional acts. We have watched mothers die inside and siblings lose their desire to live, as evil spirited men and women have had their way with them. Many of us have questioned the Holy Spirit; asking, 'Why, God? Why must evil have such a free hand at pulling the very souls from helpless children? How is it that evil can laugh in our faces as we come to sit at the feet of so many victims and attempt to comfort them without being seen or heard? How is it that evil can possess a man or woman and let them have their way with the good and yet ... we cannot enter a good man and come to the aid of the helpless?

"It is truly unfair that children like little Sissy Williams must fight off not only the sick and demented men and women of these times, but they must also suffer the evils that have existed since time began. Alone, they plead with us through the nights. Abandoned, they cry night after night, year after year. It is no wonder that most of them give up; that most of them drop their heads, their hands and their hearts because we don't, can't or won't come to their aid.

"We stand here humbly before you. Give us your ear. Listen to our plea. We want to do more than try to heal their spiritual wounds. We want to avenge the wrongs visited upon them. Please let us combat the acts perpetrated against them. Why can't we begin to prevent, rather than nurse their injuries? There is a growing outbreak of abominations against the innocence of children." Ozz paused, waiting for one of the senior angels to respond.

"We understand your frustrations. It is not God who has set the pace of the spread of this disease, it is man and his lust to be a god," responded one of the angels.

"No, we realize it is not God who has spread this disease, but it seems that the Almighty does not condemn these evil acts as they occur. It seems that He chooses to condemn the victim. Those who yield to the temptation and violate these children go on through life as an ordinary man or woman until their day of forgiveness or their day of judgment. But, the child who has been molested, often before the age of five, remains torn inside forever. The child may grow up thinking, 'God doesn't care.' When they think this, they also might come to the conclusion that maybe what is being done to them is acceptable," Chism responded.

"You have no right to question the Almighty or to judge evil or innocence. You are destined to serve mankind and the Almighty and to keep order on earth and in heaven. Only God knows all the answers to questions such as these. You cannot cross the boundaries set by God. No human can know of the existence of angels. No angel can speak to humans without the consent of God. It is simply forbidden," the second senior angel declared.

"Has God himself said this?" asked Ozz. There was no response. "Maybe the time is at hand. Maybe we are being summoned to weed the garden."

"Show us, and let us hear the pleas of an innocent child. Bring us the one who has laughed and we shall take the act itself before God. But, I must caution you that the evil ways that mankind has conjured up will not go away easily. There will be an outcry for the right to exist in the hearts of men. Acts of cruelty are justified through the supposed Holy works of God.

"The case can be stated that mankind has been seeded with the desire and ability to do as he pleases. Humans have selfish hearts that fuel the want for pleasure and the overwhelming yearning for sinful acts," one of the archangels said.

Another spoke quickly and directly to Ozz and Chism. "People in the world today have chosen to worship all manner of things and embrace all sorts of beliefs, all while they claim to love and worship the one true God. All of mankind has gone astray.

"God will not hear the cries of mankind because they have not been directed toward Him. When mankind awakens and asks of God in one voice, then will He answer and reclaim what is His. It is better for man not to pray at all than to direct his prayers to the ears a God of their choosing.

"However, the pleas of innocent children will no longer fall on deaf ears. Obviously, you and Chism have chosen to hear their cries. May God be with the both of you; but remember the hearts of men rule the earth. All the angels of the world will fall short without God."

The senior angels stood silently, awaiting any other comments that Ozz and Chism might make. Ozz slowly raised his head as if to speak and then quickly lowered it again as if he had changed his mind.

"Out with it. You seem to be holding something back," said one of the senior angels.

Ozz again raised his head, and looked sadly into the eyes of the senior angel.

"Speak your feelings," the angel urged.

"I am suddenly saddened by something that took place as we've been standing here before you," said Ozz. "Please come with me on what humans call a short walk."

The senior angels nodded to each other in agreement and followed Ozz and Chism on a journey to the human realm. They left the holy place and opened a white gate that led to a small funeral home on Lincoln Avenue, in the eastern section of Pittsburgh.

The funeral home was a one-story converted house with peeling paint and old wood windows. It was in need of a caretaker, which the owners probably couldn't afford. As they walked up the long sidewalk and into the double doors, they were greeted by a chalk written service notice that read: 10 a.m. funeral service for Lisa Staples.

They entered a short corridor with an exceptionally low ceiling. On their right was a floor to ceiling mural Jesus Christ, pictured with long flowing blond hair and blue eyes. He was kneeling beside a rock and gazing up into the heavens with a pleading look on his face.

They went through a set of double doors, and found themselves facing about fifty folding chairs lined up in neat rows. Three humans faced the angels as they entered. One was apparently an usher and two others were an elderly couple quietly sitting and waiting the rest of their family to arrive. The time showing on a wall clock behind them read 10 a.m. The group of angels turned to their left, and there, sitting up on a two-step stage sat a small child-sized casket adorned in white silk and lace. At the head of the casket were two child angels weeping.

"It is a joy to have her among us but it was not her time," said one of the angels to Ozz. "She still yearns for her mother, even as she is prepared for the journey."

The four-year-old black girl's body lay lifeless in the small coffin, as the angels appeared to view it.

"She is so beautiful," said one of the senior angels. "How is it that she was taken before her time?" he asked.

Ozz answered, "She was alone on a playground when a twenty-five year old male gained her confidence and persuaded her to follow him into a nearby wooded. Once there, he forcibly and violently raped the child in ways that we are ashamed to say. And then he decided that she might be able to identify him later, so he wrapped the sleeves of the girl's shirt around her neck and choked her until she was lifeless. That poor trusting child never stood the a chance of surviving his assault."

Ozz motioned for the others to follow him. He took them to an apartment building on the West End near the home of the dead child and a short distance from the playground. They entered one of the apartments to find four men drinking and laughing as they watched a Steeler football game. They shouted their opinions of who would win or loose the game and just how and why.

The phone rang and a female voice on the line instructed one of the men to turn to channel 4 for the news. To the objections of the others, the man answering the phone pointed the channel changer and clicked to a local news story, *"A local four year old West End child was found murdered in the woods near the park on Thursday. She had been raped and strangled. The police need your help in solving this crime. Anyone who has any information, please call the crime line and bring this criminal to justice."*

"Damn," he said. "Turn that shit off. We missin' the game. Dat wasn't nobody but some whitey. You know dey do kids and everythin' else. Turn the damn game back on."

One of the men sat quietly and sipped on his Iron City beer. He suddenly snapped out of his short trance, sat up and leaned forward toward the TV set.

"Get on wit da game, man. Dat's what we here for. Damn dat cold-blooded bullshit, dat'l take you out of yo high," he said while laughing loudly and putting up his hand for a high five.

The channel was clicked back to the game. "Dat's what I'm talkin' about," the child killer said.

The angels stood looking at the child's rapist and murderer as laughter and celebration filled the room.

"I've seen enough of this," said one of the elders.

"Please come with me, one more stop. Please?" Ozz asked

They nodded in agreement, and walked into a back room attached to a barn in Fayette County, Pa.

Curled up into a ball was a small white boy. He weighed about 50 pounds, and his skin was pale from lack of sunlight. He lay there alone in the dark with his eyes wide open, looking hopelessly lost.

"He is ten years old," Ozz said. "He has been kept in this small room for nearly five years and never allowed to go outside. He is alive — he thinks, he dreams, he hungers for prayers to be answered. Yet, year after year, he lies here waiting for the mercy of death. He was abducted from a grocery store after he strayed from his mother. She has been searching for him since that day."

"Why is he here?" asked a senior angel.

"Come with me," Ozz said. They walked from the barn to a wood frame house about 200 yards away. At the table was a bearded man in his early sixties, a woman, probably a few years younger, another adult male about forty years old and two females in their late thirties. They all sat at their dinner table as the father bowed his head in prayer.

"All mighty God," he prayed. "Thank you for the food we are about to receive. Bless us, Oh Lord, with your kindness and patience and forgive us for our sins. We share at this table the bounty you have made possible. Amen."

"Amen," they all repeated as they let go of each other's hand to begin their meal.

"Why is the child in the barn?" one of the senior angels asked Ozz again.

"The son brought the child home to teach him to help with the chores and to be mothered by his childless sisters. When they realized someone might see him and recognize him from the many posters that were put up all over the county, they decided to hide him until he got older.

"The child, sickened from a broken heart, would not eat the scraps they threw him. Because they are Christians, they could not take his life. So, they decided to let him die a natural death instead. When he finally dies, they plan to bury him so no one will ever know. The boy doesn't know how to die, so he has suffered all these years while his mother still searches for him with unending hope."

"Bring the child's spirit with us. Let us leave here. We will see no more; these sights are making us angry., What manner of people are these who harm the helpless? What has possessed this human world?" the senior angel asked.

Chism stepped forward and responded, "These are the types of human adults that have been cursed with an infection of evil that can surge into a soul at any moment and loom huge and uncontrollable. An evil that comes to and from their hearts so quickly that some cannot recognize themselves from one moment to the next."

"Who is responsible for these acts?" one archangel asked.

"The one who commits them is responsible. They are like a trickling stream of water that is more often than not making its way to a projected destination. The stream is often a lifeline for all that are in need of it, but suddenly and without warning it can become a raging river, strong enough to change the face of the earth. Before it can be labeled as a river of fury, it becomes a harmless trickling stream again. It is both a friendly stream and raging river. Some humans are the same. They are a river of rage that lures their victims by acting like a gentle stream."

"How can we prevent actions by this type of human?" the archangel asked.

"We cannot. They are deceptive by nature; many times they do not even recognize the onslaught of their own lust. We can only be extremely aware of the damage they cause if they are left unwatched. If we are lax in our duties, they abuse every unsuspecting victim they can and then quickly revert to being harmless so we cannot spot them," answered Chism.

"How can we begin to recognize the difference between a gentle man and an evil man?"

"Since they can be one and the same, we must know that just as a stream can become a raging river, a man can become evil without notice. Consequently all men should be watched carefully. It would be much wiser to treat a stream as a potential river, than to assume a sleeping river is just a stream.

"To you," Chism turned and addressed another angel, "the highest form of angels, I make a more serious presentation on behalf of Ozz. You once warned us that being assigned to comfort the children of the land would be a difficult task, yet one that would bring joy. I have yet to experience that joy and find that we are engaged in a constant battle against evil. I believe it is our destiny to fight this plague; we are the only cure.

"Many times I have looked into the eyes and mind of children, and each time I see the same yearning passion to give and receive love. And then suddenly and without warning, the child is jolted by the unexpected intrusion of evil. They cry out and look to the spirit that actually carried them into this life, but it's not there to help them.

"We have been chosen to protect these souls until the storm has subsided and to see to it that the flesh doesn't overwhelm and smother their spirits. You say there will be times of tribulation that will pierce the outer limits of their hearts, but nothing will stand between God and his children. You say worry not, the time of fear will be short. The cloak of flesh is the protective shield against that which might penetrate the spirit and soul. Our engagement has turned into a struggle against a force that has found a way to inflict injury while the flesh is young and vulnerable and the soul is not fully protected. Are we to let this plague take its toll or are we to stand up and merge with flesh and blood and turn this tide of humiliation?

"No spirit is safe from evil. The intruder has learned to attack the youngest and most vulnerable. From the side of us that is human I beg you, let me lead the counterattack against this evil. From the side of us that is Godly, allow us to keep our memory of God. This I beg of you. If not now, when? Tomorrow, for humans, can never be reached. Let us start heading back this very moment. From the mouths of babes has come the plea. Their plea is justified, for they have been violated. Since what I have said is true, I ask that you give us the right to choose. What is your answer?' asked Chism.

After a quiet pause came the answer, "No ... let them find their way back without your help. The moment you become flesh, you will lose your memory of God. It always has been this way, so it will always be. Again I say, an angel is to heal only the soul. Man must combat the evil of man. We will never be far away from them. If you still choose to stand for them, you must become a man without memory of your angelic self."

"Then humbly, I say to you, I look forward to the day that I may become a man," Ozz boldly said.

# CHAPTER 15

Floyd picked up Henry from the hospital and headed back toward South Street. "I hope you wasn't messin' wit my wife while I was laid up. Was you?" he asked jokingly.

"Naw," answered Floyd with a big wide grin on his face. "You know I wouldn't do dat."

"Go by Holy Temple Church. I wanna get a number from the Bishop. I feel lucky. Then we need to go by the numbers man so I can play twenty dollars worth."

"Okay, but you gotta buy me some gas, nigga. I ain't gonna be just ridin' you around for free," said Floyd.

"No wait, let's stop by Sam's first. I need a drink. Then we can go by the church, its right on the way," Henry instructed.

"You gonna buy me a drink, too?" Floyd asked.

"Yeah," said Henry. "Just get us there."

After a few drinks, they headed over to the church.

"Hey, Rev," Floyd said, as he greeted the Bishop.

"Hello, gentlemen. I haven't seen you two in a while. I don't know if God still recognizes either of you," said Bishop Jones his effeminate voice.

"Yo, Rev," said Henry, "I know I ain't been around, but I sure need a good number to play. Now I know you can take care of me like that, can't cha?"

"You gentlemen should be ashamed. I haven't seen you in so long and the first thing you ask for is a number. Lordy, what's this world coming to?" the Bishop joked.

"Come on, Rev," Floyd cajoled.

"Oh, you know I'm going to take care of you guys. Come on into my office," he said while gesturing for them to follow.

They walked towards the rear of the huge church, passing a group of children that were practicing new dance steps in the play area. Bishop Jones's church doubled as a school for young children, as well as a place to buy a "hot" number from the Lord.

"Hmm, I see you still got all these young virgins goin' to yo church, Rev. I don't know how ya keep your hands off them sweet little things," said Floyd.

The three men came to a stop and watched the children dance.

"Um-um-um," Floyd kept saying, indicating his lustful desire.

Henry just stood watching until his eyes locked onto a small young girl who had been watching the others but appeared to be too shy to participate. "Who's the little girl in the red skirt?" Henry asked the Bishop.

"Come on now, guys. You fellas didn't come here for that. At least not this time," said the Bishop.

"No, I'm just sayin', she's so cute," said Henry.

"She sho is," Floyd agreed. "Rev you gotta fix us up with a couple of these young'uns. You used to take care of us. You still got dat little room behind the bathroom where you used to watch da little boys tinkle?" Floyd asked.

"You know it. Everybody needs a little visual pleasure sometime," said the Bishop.

"Take us back there, Rev. We need a little treat ourselves," Floyd stated.

"I thought you came for numbers. Both of you got your minds sidetracked to some young stuff," the Bishop reminded them.

"Come on, Rev," Floyd pleaded.

"Oh, all right but just for a moment," said the Bishop.

Ozz and Chism watched as the three sick men found their way to a small space between the walls of the restrooms.

"Do you think this church and Reverend Jones are at the root of this evil circle of humans?" Ozz asked Chism.

"I don't know. Look at them. All three of them turn my stomach. Let's bide our time until we know who is the evil one, then we will strike. Maybe this time we will succeed," said Ozz.

After Henry and Floyd received their lucky number from the Bishop and had their fun watching the children dress and undress, they continued their journey toward South Street. Both men were sexually aroused and both had little Sissy on their minds.

"You don't think I know bout what you been doin' to little Sissy, do ya?" Floyd casually asked Henry.

"What you talkin' about?" asked Henry innocently.

"You know what I'm talkin' about. I seen you doin' Sissy when she wasn't much more than a baby," said Floyd.

"Dat's my baby. I do what I wanna do," said Henry.

"Well you dun a good job, 'cause she takes care of old Floyd, too."

"What, what you sayin', Floyd? You done messed with my Sissy?" he asked.

"Yeah, nigga, you know I did, 'cause I seen you watchin', just like I seen Hazel watchin' me a lotta times."

"I'll kill you, nigga, if you ever touch my baby again," said Henry.

"How you gonna kill somebody? Your heart'll stop on you just like dat!" he said, snapping his fingers. "Anyway, ain't nothin' wrong wit it. It keeps men like you an me young."

"Yeah, well you best not touch her again, Floyd," Henry threatened.

"Okay, but don't ask me about da two young'uns I got over on Kelly Street. They momma's always drunk and da kids don't tell nobody 'cause they scared. I got 'em too scared to tell. They just takes care of Floyd. They ain't like them ole-ass women. These is virgins.

"You know the Rev said children is virgins 'til they reach eleven, then they hoes like da mommas. These is young virgins who done learned to do what ya tell 'em. We bulls, me an you, we bulls. They need men like us to teach 'em how ta please they men when they grow up. They'll thank us someday cause we taught 'em good."

"How old they be?" asked Henry.

"One's six and one's seven."

"Do they scream and make a lot of noise?" Asked Henry.

"A little, but we can just take da momma some wine and she'll pass out. If they wake her up, she'll tear they little asses up wit a belt."

"Let's pick her up a bottle of wine," said Henry, while giving Floyd a high five.

Henry and Floyd entered the back door of the home on Kelly Street just before dark. "I got a key to all my women's houses," Floyd proudly announced with his typical grin. They climbed a short flight of steps and went through a second door that separated the living room from the kitchen. To their right were the two young girls. They were watching cartoons and never looked up at the two men as they went into the kitchen.

When they got there, the mother was sitting at the table talking on the phone. She had a cigarette in her hand and a saucer full of butts was in front of her, indicating she'd been on the phone for a while. She took one more sip from her glass before telling whoever she was talking to that she had to go.

"Hi, baby," she said, greeting Floyd, who grinned at her.

"This my friend, Henry," he said. "We came over to have a few drinks wit ya, baby. We wanna have ourselves a little good time," he said and shimmied his shoulders.

The three of them sat at the kitchen table and began to talk about the good old days. While the two men drank a small amount of beer, the young alcoholic mother guzzled the free wine, filling glass after glass until she was fall down drunk.

Floyd looked over at Henry and tapped him on the leg. "She ready to go," he said. "Come on, girl, Floyd gonna take you up stairs and tuck you in."

The woman slightly opened her eyes and said, "You gonna do more than tuck me in, 'cause I'm ready for you." She giggled as Floyd stood up and helped her to her feet.

"Henry, why don't you go in and watch some TV wit the children," he said, and winked. "I'll take care of dis, then I be back down in a hurry. You make sure you save me some of dat good stuff in there," he said gesturing with his head in the direction of the living room.

Henry walked into the living room where both of the girls had fallen to sleep with the TV still on. One of them had curled up in one corner of the couch and the other on the opposite side. Henry sat down between the two.

Within half an hour, Floyd had successfully put the children's mother to sleep and hurried back down stairs to join Henry and the girls. The two men, with hearts of slime, took advantage of their victims until they both lay exhausted. They had also succeeded in bringing themselves even closer to the angels' wrath.

# CHAPTER 16

This was a rare Saturdays for Sissy. There had been no nighttime visit from Floyd, and her father was having chest pains again. She had a long day playing like any ordinary eight-year-old. She played the game of school, in which she pretended to be the teacher. She taught and disciplined her brothers until they got bored and went out to play in the streets.

Sissy spent the rest afternoon playing with her Easy Bake Oven, and preparing sweet cakes to give to her mother. Toward the end of the day, she sat out on the front porch listening to the laughter of other children down the block. She was much too shy to make friends. Sometimes she felt attracted to other kids her own age that jumped rope on the sidewalk a few houses down, but she seldom ventured too close to them. She had convinced herself that other kids didn't like her, so she pretty much stayed to herself, finding security putting her thumb in her mouth. She was content watching the others play and have fun.

Most of the time, she did chores and tried to avoid her father and Floyd or any other grown up males because she assumed they had the same mindset as Floyd and her dad. She often wondered if all the other little girls had nights of fear and late night visits from the adults in their household. Maybe it was just her, and this was her punishment for doing something wrong. Although she couldn't remember ever doing anything that warranted all the sadness she had endured, she often thought maybe she hadn't cleaned the kitchen well enough or folded the clothes right or not vacuumed the carpet or any of the day to day chores that seemed to be set aside for just her.

She summoned her imaginary guardian angels nearly every day. Most of the time she feared for them. She feared that Floyd would hurt them or her dad would beat them as he did her mother on a regular basis. She summoned them, but she kept them out of harm's way. She wouldn't bring them to her while Floyd was in the house. She knew she would never be forgiven if they were hurt.

They were always so soft-spoken and kind. They often said to her "Don't worry, someday you will be like Cinderella in the storybook and you will be saved by a hero. A hero who will build a fence around you so no one will get in unless you want them to. You will be a special eight-year-old with pretty clothes and shiny black shoes. You will also send your hero out to help all the little girls who are lonely and can't find a reason to be happy." These were her friends, and though they couldn't protect her, she had done a good job protecting them.

# CHAPTER 17

"Where does this evil against children dwell?" asked Ozz "Is it the house that Sissy lives in? Is it the dark alleys that separate the streets? Is it the bishop who sells numbers from God? Is it the community? The city? The state? The country or the world? Is it in the universe and on into the heavens? Is it the uncles and fathers like Henry and Floyd? Is it the uncaring mothers? Is it the seeds of Satan or the sickness of the devil?

"If you and I find the source of evil can we, or rather are we, strong enough to deal with it? The laws that govern us plainly read, 'we are to bring comfort to the injured hearts and assure them that God has sent His Son who will recognize even the smallest merits of good'. We have engaged ourselves to sting not only the hands of evil, but to destroy the vessels they are using to harm children. These vessels are men and women who have hollowed their hearts and souls to make room for the works of evil.

"I guess the question is, if we destroy the vessel, does the evil move on to the next vessel? Also, what becomes of the vessel if evil abandons it on its own? Does compassion return? Can a man or woman turn his or her life around and find Christ? Even if they can, what becomes of the child who has been affected for life with sadness and confusion? What redemption is there for those whose lives were cut short?

"When all is said and done, and actions are weighed, there can only be one fair answer. We must act against evil while evil is in the act of destruction. While it is consuming its prey, we must strike and pull it out from its roots, even if it means that the vessel must die. After all, men and women who have blinded themselves to the evil that is being done must bear a major portion of responsibility and they must face the consequences. They should be willing to give up their own lives before letting harm come to their children. 'I would die first' should be a common response to the temptation of harming a child, especially your own. Many would die or kill to protect the life of a child.

"Let's not let these vessels claim that 'the devil made them do it.' They are aware of the sick pleasures they have found in these acts. Let's let them also be aware of the sword of punishment and the payment for these God forsaken deeds. May God forgive them when the child who has been violated forgives them."

# CHAPTER 18

"Happy birthday, baby girl!"

"I'm not a baby."

"How old are you now, six or seven?"

"No, Daddy, I'm nine. You know I'm nine," Sissy said to her father.

"What you want for yo birthday present, little girl?"

"Daddy you always ask but you never buy me anything," she answered.

"Well what you want? I didn't say I was gonna get it. I just want to know what you want. Anyway, yo momma take care of that stuff," Henry said, smiling.

"I think Momma's gonna make me a cake. If she does, I want my nine candles lit. When I blow them out, I'm gonna make the best wish of my life."

"What you gonna wish for, little girl? Somethin' for Daddy?"

"No! I'm not tellin' anyone."

"Well, it won't come true unless you tell yo daddy."

"That's not true. If you tell someone your wish, that means it won't come true," Sissy said.

"I know what you wishin' for," Henry said. "You wishin' for new clothes ain't you?"

"No, I want somethin' real special for Momma."

"For yo momma? Why you want somethin' for her? Come here, give yo daddy a hug."

"No, Daddy, I don't want to."

"Ah, girl, come here. I don't want nothin' but a hug right now 'cause I got to go."

Sissy was beginning to devise ways of keeping her father away from her by avoiding him, especially when there was no one else at home. As for Floyd, there was no way to avoid him. He was a terror. Everyone in the household, including Henry, was afraid of Floyd.

"Come on, baby, I said give yo daddy a hug," he said in a stern voice.

Sissy looked in both directions and found she was without an exit from the room, this was the very thing she had learned to avoid. She slowly tried to position herself closer to the door by continuing to talk to her daddy, but he reached out and grabbed her before she could get away.

"Come here, baby," he said when he already had her in his grasp. He took his hug and pulled her onto his lap as he sat down on the living room chair. Henry had decided not to leave after all. After having his way with her despite her pleading, experienced another bout of heart pains.

This time Sissy didn't call out to anyone to help him. She grabbed her clothing and ran upstairs. "There's nothing wrong with you, daddy. I wish you would die," she said as she slammed her bedroom door. Like so many times before, she cried until her little eyes ran dry. "I hate him! I hate him so much," she said out loud.

And like so many times before, Ozz was furious. In an instant he was by her side.

"Where were you?" she asked Ozz.

"I was coming to you but I could only come when you— You can see me?" Ozz asked in surprise.

"Yes, I told you that before. I can see you, and I can hear you, too."

Ozz was amazed by Sissy's ability to see him. He'd been involved in the lives of thousands of children and none of them had ever been able to see or hear him or any of the other angels, either. Only through God himself was an angel's voice or visual appearance permitted.

"How long have you been able to see and hear me?" he asked.

"For as long as I can remember," Sissy answered.

"Why have you never spoken to me before?"

"Because I was afraid Floyd would hear you and take you and angel Chism away from me."

"People can't harm us, little girl, and we have yet to find a way to harm evil people, even for the sake of precious children like you. As I speak to you, I'm angry at the trickery and deceptiveness your father uses to violate you, his own flesh and blood."

Sissy calmly reverted back to her childlike demeanor, and sadly said, "It's my birthday. I wanted him to leave me alone. Just once on my birthday I wanted to be happy like other kids. I didn't even want a present; I just wanted to be nine. I hoped when I was nine things would be different. Every time I get a year older, I hope I can have a happy birthday and that it would last for the rest of my life. I'm not happy now, though. Will I be happy when I'm ten?" she asked innocently.

Ozz was speechless.

"I guess that means no. Why do I have to make my daddy happy? Why can't I make my mommy happy, and why can't my birthday be my happy day?"

Ozz stood up and began to walk toward the door. He didn't know how to respond to the child. He didn't have the answers to any of her questions.

Downstairs, Henry called out, "Sissy, come help Daddy."

"I'll help him," said Ozz.

"No, don't go down there, he'll take you away from me. Daddy and Floyd will take you and Chism and I won't have anyone in the world," she pleaded.

Ozz listened, but descended the staircase anyway. Henry was stretched out on the chair, still naked from the waist down. He was holding his chest in pain, just as he had done so many times before.

"Sissy!" he yelled again, "Daddy's in pain."

Ozz prevented Sissy from hearing his voice. "Not this time, Henry. "This time you'll save yourself or die," Ozz said, although he knew Henry couldn't hear him. "You can't hear me, but I can hear you, Henry. I can hear you moan like a coward. I can hear you cry out to the very child you just raped, deceived and threatened. A child that believed her submission to you would protect her world from your vengeance. She can't hear you now. She can't be drained of purity to save your stinking life. I can't help you, Henry. No one can hear my voice. I can't call out for you or lift you up. I can't even stomp your guts out as I wish to do. I can only watch you suffer. I will watch without pity or compassion. All I feel for you is the forbidden hate that has grown in me toward cowards like you who rape and abuse helpless children."

"Don't hurt him! Don't hurt my daddy. He's going to do better; he's going to see that I'm a good girl. He'll be sorry and then be better." Sissy, shouted. She'd walked up behind Ozz without drawing his attention, and startled him.

"Go get Miss Judy from next door, tell her I need help," Henry instructed Sissy.

Ozz stood blocking the door as Sissy looked up at him. "Please, angel Ozz, he's going to do better. I promise," said Sissy.

Ozz stood aside as he looked over at Henry who was smiling and looking directly into his eyes. Ozz heard the loud voice of laughter echo in his mind, just as it had before.

Sissy ran out the front door to get help for her father so she could save him once again from the jaws of death.

"No," Ozz said. "No not this time."

"God, don't let me die," Henry said while still clutching his heart.

Ozz lifted his hand and drew in all the air in the room, depriving the coward of oxygen.

"You are not to kill a human," a voice from behind him said.

Ozz continued to draw the air into his mouth and Henry slumped over, unconscious.

"Stop! Stop now!" said Chism shouted. "This is wrong. You cannot kill and remain an angel."

Ozz paused as Henry began grasping for air while coughing weakly.

"Let him die, but don't kill him," Chism said.

"Men like him don't die," said Ozz. "They just live until they are forgiven."

"So be it, Ozz. We can't carry it through no matter what we feel," Chism said.

"He's no good. He's selfish and cruel and gathers his strength from the innocence of children," said Ozz.

As the two angels spoke, an ambulance arrived and two men entered the room with the neighbor, Ms. Judy, leading the way.

"To let him die will not put the fire out that burns so painfully in my heart," said Ozz.

"I know. I, too, desperately want to see him die; but not by your hand. I've come to the realization that it is not our place to kill," said Chism.

Again, laughter loudly rang out, and only Ozz and Chism could hear it.

Both angels, turned their attention to one of the ambulance attendants, who said, "He's dead."

"Oh, my God!" the neighbor exclaimed. "That poor child is going to be so upset. She was her father's favorite and he must've practically died in her arms. Oh, my God!"

"He's not dead," Ozz said,

"I know, but they think he is, let's watch and see," said Chism.

The medics began trying to revive him. They worked for nearly half an hour trying to get the dead man to breathe, to no avail. "He's gone, we'll have to call the coroner's office," one said to the other.

"He's not dead." Ozz repeated.

"They said he is, so he is," said Chism.

Henry's heart had slowed to an undetectable pace, barely keeping him alive.

"Let's go to Sissy," Ozz said as Chism followed him towards the exit door.

Ozz and Chism entered the neighbor's house and found Sissy patiently sitting with her hands folded in her lap. She was looking up at the two angels as she spoke.

"My daddy's not dead; he just can't open his eyes," she said.

"I haven't had an opportunity to tell you that not only can she definitely hear us, she can see us, too," Ozz told Chism.

"But that's not possible," said Chism.

"Yes it is, because she can."

"She knows her father's not dead?"

"Apparently, but don't ask me how."

"Speak to her, I want to see for myself," said Chism.

"I see you," said Sissy.

Chism came closer and asked, "What do we look like, little girl?"

"I don't know," she said. "You look like God."

"Can you describe Ozz to me?" Chism asked.

"Well," she said and paused, while looking directly at Ozz, "his skin is like chocolate milk, only smoother. He has bushy eyebrows that are black and silky. His eyes are big and his eye balls move constantly and they show stories."

"What do you mean, they show stories?"

"I can see a lot of things when I look into his eyes, and sometimes he talks with them without moving his mouth. Sometimes, I hear him when I can't see him at all. Sometimes I hear him crying because I think he's afraid of my daddy and Floyd, so I don't let him come when they're around me."

"Do we look like ordinary people to you?"

"Yes, like God, only not as bright."

"Have you seen God, Sissy?"

"Only in your eyes, when you're afraid He's going to be mad at you for being bad," she answered.

"Touch me," said Ozz,

"I can't. I can't touch you because I'll get you dirty. … My daddy's not dead, you know."

The coroner put Henry William's body into a bag and zipped it closed. They put him on a stretcher and carried his body to a waiting van. As they approached the van, little Sissy ran up to them.

"No!" she screamed, "My daddy's not dead; he just can't talk. Take him out of that bag!" she demanded.

"Please hold the child back," the coroner said to Ms. Judy.

"Come on, baby, we've got to find your mother," Ms. Judy said to Sissy.

"No! Miss Judy, he's not dead; he just can't talk," she repeated as they loaded his body into the van.

Sissy looked towards Ozz and Chism for help. "Tell them he's not dead. Please!"

The coroner's van pulled into the city morgue on Ross Street in downtown Washington. As the two men got out of the vehicle, they were greeted by a third man who told them he'd just received a call from the Dormont police department. There'd been a murder suicide. A man killed his three children and his wife, then turned the gun on himself. "We need to get over there immediately," the man told the others.

"Okay, let's get this stiff inside the fridge and we'll get right back on the road."

After putting Henry Williams into a refrigerated drawer, they tied a tag on his big toe and headed to the scene of the multiple murders.

When the door slammed on Henry, the force of the air caused him to gasp and take in a deep breath. He was alive. Henry was lying there on his back, not quite awake. He felt like he was just coming out of a dream.

He began to stroke himself into an erection as he began to come more and more out of his sleep. "Sissy," he called out, "come here, baby. Daddy's still in need."

He opened his eyes and found himself in complete darkness. He tried to raise his hand off of his crouch and hit the steel ceiling of the drawer. He was startled by the fact that something was above him. He tried to sit up and smashed his nose and forehead against the steel ceiling. He felt blood trickle down his nose.

Henry began to panic, "Sissy!" he screamed. "Hazel, where are you? What's goin' on here?" He again attempted to raise his hands, this time to wipe away the blood that was running down his face. He began to breathe heavily as the air in the stainless steel chamber was used up.

He had about six inches of space between his chest and the top of the drawer His shoulders were pressed against the walls. His head was against the deepest part of the drawer and his feet could barely touch the other side of the drawer. It was pitch black and air-tight. He started to feel the coldness of the refrigerated steel.

"Help me!" he screamed. "Help me!" Needless to say, Henry Williams was no longer erect, and he no longer thought about abusing his nine-year-old daughter. His lust had turned to fear.

"Sissy. Oh, my God, Sissy! Wake me up from this nightmare. Somebody help me!" He began to struggle and use up the remaining air still locked in the chamber. Henry was dying. He could hear thousands upon thousands of voices. Some were screaming, some were talking loudly, and others were faint. He heard laughter and many languages that he'd never heard before.

"Shut up!" he yelled. "Shut up!" Suddenly all the voices stopped and it instantly became quiet. Henry Williams listened for any familiar sound or voice. There was nothing. There was no sound at all in the total darkness.

"Stop, Daddy. Please stop!"

"Sissy, is that you, baby? Help daddy find his way. I'll never bother you again, baby — I promise. I'll always, from now on, be better, baby. Just get daddy out of this- this darkness. Help me! Somebody, help me!" The laughter began again and it was louder and louder as they continued to laugh.

The lack of oxygen in the drawer was causing him to heave in an attempt to draw in any oxygen that was left. His chest began to cave-in against his lungs. The air was gone. Silence came again. Henry, for some reason, began to count. "Ten, nine, eight, seven six, five, four," he tried again to pound his hands against the sides at his waist, "three, two, one."

When he got to one, he began to cry, "Oh, my God, please get me out ... of...heeere..." His bad heart exploded into pain as he tried to cry out again. Finally the drawer door was opened and light came flooding in. A coroner assigned to prepare his dead body had pulled the drawer out into the well-lit room.

*Yes,* Henry thought, *I'm saved!*

"Well, big fell a, its time for your bath," the coroner said. "Then we'll get you all prettied up for your family to see. But first, I've got to drain all those nasty bodily fluids." He inserted a draining tube into Henry's neck, then said,

"Once we're done here, we'll send you over to be embalmed for your last journey."

Henry was frantic. He believed he was visibly moving his eyes, his mouth and his hands but in reality they were as still as the metal slab he was lying on. *I'm not dead!* he thought. *Why can't he see that I'm not dead! God help me! I'm not dead!"*

The coroner finished his work, turned off the lights and left the room as Henry screamed, but only in his mind. In a few moments the last of his blood had slowly dripped from his throat. Henry continued to think he was alive. His mind raced forward with hope that someone would realize he was lying here and just couldn't move. He had no way of knowing that he was truly dead. Again he silently screamed and begged as the hand of death squeezed and twisted every vital organ of his body. Henry was lifeless and yet in his mind it was only a matter of someone hearing his cries and coming to his rescue.

*What I would give for a glimpse of light or the sound of a familiar voice or to be touched by a living soul once more, just once more. Any thing, any body, any where,* he thought. Henry's life had come to an end without his knowledge of an ending. From here on, time would have no meaning for him. He was finally a man with no evil in his veins and no one to harm. Evil had moved on in search of another selfish place to dwell, while he relived the agony of hopelessness again and again.

# CHAPTER 19

"We are gathered here to pay our last respects to a good man, a family man, a loving father and husband," said the Bishop as he raised his head and looked out into the crowd of mourning people. "Henry Williams was the kind of man we all could like. Can I get an Amen?"

"Amen," repeated the crowd of people, "Amen."

"He is no longer suffering down here with us. Now he is with the Lord. Amen. I see his family sitting out there in grief. Hazel, his sons and- and- and- his daughter. If he could speak now, he would tell you all, 'Don't worry about me, 'cause I'm in a better place now.' Amen. He would say, 'It's been a long journey but I'm here now.' Amen. Can I get an Amen?"

"Amen," repeated the crowd of mourners.

Floyd sat there listening to the Bishop. *Bullshit!* he thought to himself. *Henry was my friend but he wasn't no damn good man. If he anywhere, he in hell where he belong.*

Hazel was crying. The memories of her husband had already begun to fade, but she knew what was expected so she shed tears to make a good impression. With her head down, she glanced over at Floyd. *At last,* she thought, *No more of him beatin' and kickin' me. Now I can love Floyd without him buttin' in.*

Sissy sat next to her mother. She never took her eyes off of her daddy. She thought he would be getting up any minute now. She felt his presence and she knew he was still here. Sissy looked over at Floyd sitting on the other side of her mother. He glanced back at her with an affectionate grin that she had never seen before. It was the same look of affection her father had learned to wear when he had intentions of winning her trust. It was a look that always went from kind to evil, from sweet words to violent profanity, from a gentle touch to a blind rage of pain. Like at the end, when he always seemed to want her to say thank you, as if there could have possibly been some level of pleasure in the experience for her.

He, her daddy, was sick with selfishness and evil, but somehow she loved him anyway. Sissy had no way to know what a true father-daughter relationship should be. Henry was the only father she knew. Compared to Floyd, he was a gallant savior, and now he was gone.

Floyd had wasted no time positioning himself as the new lion. He could now add another household to his fold. Again, she looked over at Floyd as he spoke to her mother. *He has absorbed my father's evil soul,* she thought. *He has taken his existence and made it a part of his own. I can feel it. Somehow he and my daddy have become one.*

"Oh, God Almighty," said Ozz, "we have watched an evil man die, just to join with another. He's still here. His body is dead but his source of pleasure and his reason for existing continues to thrive all around us. He's dead but the disease is alive and well. On one hand, some of the terror for Sissy has ended but on the other Floyd has the newly found convenience of torturing Sissy without having to wait for Henry to leave home."

"I don't know," said Chism, "it seems as though Sissy has no possibility of finding peace or true affection. The long-standing cult of child molesters has claimed her as their own. Even if we devise a plan to make Floyd pay with his stinking life, there will always be others who recognize her as one of God's children has had her innocence. We have failed her but she's strong. If we can help her reach adulthood, maybe fate will bless her by letting her forget and ultimately forgive those of us who have let it happen. Let's leave this forbidden temple these people believe is a house of God," said Chism.

"No," said Ozz, "I'm going to stay with her for a while. I want to hear what the Bishop has to say in his heart about the collective lives of those such as Henry. I want to see for myself how the so-called Christians manage to 'amen' the likes of Henry Williams into heaven, or should I say the heaven they have perceived."

"Can I get an Amen?" the Bishop asked again.

"Amen," echoed the mourners.

"You see, none of us is perfect. None of us have obeyed the Lord one hundred percent of the time, but the Bible says, 'Let he who has not sinned cast the first stone.' Can I get an Amen?"

"Amen."

"The Bible says, 'Ask and you shall be forgiven.' Can I get an Amen?"

"Amen."

"The Bible says, 'Only Christ can live without sin.' Can I get an Amen?"

"Amen."

"Henry Williams was my friend. He didn't always come to church like he should, but I know he kept Jesus in mind. I know he read his Bible. I know he feared the Lord, Can I get an Amen?"

"Amen."

Hazel burst into tears and Ozz wondered if it was due to sadness or joy at being rid of her abusive husband. Or was she touched by the ridiculous words of the Bishop pertaining to the man who just a few days ago had beaten her and molested several innocent children, including his own daughter?

The funeral precession moved from the church to the gravesite in the Wood St. Cemetery. The Bishop quoted the usual final words as Henry's body was lowered into the ground. Little Sissy stood behind several adults and peered from between them to watch as the casket that held her daddy was lowered into the ground.

"That concludes this service," said the Bishop. "We can all meet back at the church where a dinner will be served."

As everyone began to hurry back to their cars, Sissy found herself walking far behind her family. Ozz was floating above her and gazing around at the many headstones and huge grave markers of those who'd died before Henry Williams. He wondered how many of the dead, like Henry, should have never lived. *How many here had lived for the sole purposes of making others suffer their evil and hateful presence?* he wondered. Ozz looked down to where he assumed Sissy would be, but found her about ten yards behind him facing the gravesite of her father.

A young lady of about 25 years old was left standing alone. She was looking down into the grave and talking but Sissy couldn't hear what she was saying. Sissy walked back to the grave and stood within hearing distance of the young lady.

"I've looked forward to this day," she said as she spat down into the grave. May you enjoy all the evil that lies at the bottom of hell!" She spat again and again. "I hope you burn if there is a hell. I hope they have a place there to repay you for your sick love-like evil." She spat once more and kicked dirt and stones onto the top of his casket.

Little Sissy began to cry. She startled the young woman who thought she was there alone.

"Hey," she said, as she quickly changed her tone of voice to kindness. "What's wrong?" She bent over and wiped the tears from Sissy's face. "Sorry," she said, "I didn't mean to frighten you. What's your name, child?"

"I'm not a child," Sissy answered. "I just turned nine years old. Why are you saying mean things to my daddy?"

"I'm sorry, I didn't know you were here. I didn't mean to hurt you. You see, I know your daddy; he was my daddy, too."

Sissy stopped crying and looked up into the eyes of the lady. "Are you my sister?"

"I guess I am," said the lady.

"I hated my daddy, too, sometimes."

The young lady stood back and held out her hand for Sissy to take. Sissy put her hand into the lady's and asked, "What's your name?"

"My name is Helen. What's yours?"

"My name is Joyce but they call me Sissy," she said. Sissy smiled thinking that such a pretty lady might really be her sister, even though she wasn't sure how that could be.

Ozz knew exactly who Helen was. He'd comforted Helen on many nights, just as he did Sissy and so many others like them in an attempt to keep their souls and spirits Godly. Helen paused and turned around toward the gravesite; once more she had a glare in her eyes that indicated her hate for Henry Williams. What he had done to little Sissy was mild compared to what he'd done to her.

"Well," Helen said, "it seems like they've all gone off and left you. That was careless of them, but I guess there's so much going on that even grown-ups do silly things. How about I take you back to the Bishop's temple of doom, huh?" she asked Sissy. "Would you like that?"

"Yes."

The two of them climbed into Helen's silver Mercedes and began their drive back to the other side of Penn Avenue. Helen had grown up to be a successful landscape designer.

"How about we stop at McDonald's? Would you like that or do you want to hurry back to the church?"

"McDonald's," said Sissy.

"What's the matter little Sister; you're not afraid are you?"

"No, I'm not afraid of you, but I'm thinking of my daddy."

"Did you like your daddy a lot?" Helen asked.

"Sometimes, I think I did."

"What didn't you like about him?"

"He was bad to me."

"What do you mean, bad to you?"

Sissy didn't answer for a bit, then said, "He's not bad as Floyd."

"Who is Floyd?"

"He's a mean man and now he has my daddy's soul."

"What do you mean, Sissy?"

"Floyd hurt me and he's mean to everyone."

Helen pulled into McDonald's parking lot. She parked the car and faced Sissy, who was sitting in the passenger's seat. "What do you mean he hurts you?" she asked.

Little Sissy changed the subject. "Can I have a milkshake?"

"Come on, let's go in and see what we want to order."

After they sat down and began eating, Helen continued her questioning. "Does Floyd sometimes put his hands on you?"

Sissy didn't answer.

"Is Floyd your favorite uncle?"

"No, I hate him and he's not my uncle. He's my daddy and momma's friend."

"Oh, I see," said Helen. "When I was a little girl like you I hated when men like Floyd put their hands on me. I always wanted to tell someone what they were doing, but I was afraid to. Can I tell you, Sissy? But, you must promise not to tell anyone else. Okay?"

"I won't tell. I promise," Sissy answered.

"No, I better not tell you. I guess I'm just not brave enough. Plus you might think I'm bad."

"No I won't," said Sissy.

"No," Helen said, "I better not. Maybe when you tell me about Floyd, I'll be able to tell you my secret stories. Floyd seems like a nice gentleman that I can trust."

"No!" Sissy screamed. "He's an evil man."

"Why do you say that, little sister? Tell me."

"Because he touches my private parts and he…"

For nearly an hour Sissy told Helen all about the things Floyd and their father had done to her. In exchange, Helen told of the similar things that had happened to her as a child. Helen explained to Sissy that what had happened to the two of them was not acceptable to most people and that there were men in the world who love and respect their kinfolk and small children. She explained to Sissy that there are men that would never harm a child.

Little Sissy was relieved. She'd always thought that all little girls were going through the same things she was, but no one would tell. She knew she wouldn't dare tell, simply because no one else spoke out against her father.

After hearing what Sissy had been going through and probably still would be going through with Floyd, Helen decided she was going to do something about it. She just wasn't sure what.

"Come on, little sister, we'd better get back to the church. I'm sure they've missed you by now."

When they got back to the church, the two newly found stepsisters walked into the crowd of relatives and friends who were still paying their respects. Sissy's mother hadn't missed her at all. She was busy laughing with some folks, and looking sad for others.

"Which one is Floyd?" Helen asked Sissy.

"No-o-o, you said you wouldn't tell."

"I'm not going to say anything, I just want to know who he is. Better yet, let me guess." Helen looked around the room trying to see if she could get a feeling for the man without knowing who he was. There were at least three men that gave her a sense that they were cruel enough to rape children, and ironically one of them was Floyd. He had given himself away, not by negative vibes but by acting like the new head of the Williams family.

Floyd spotted Helen staring at him from the corner of his eye, and turned to look at her. He put an intimidating look on his face and stared directly into her eyes while he chewed his mouth full of food. When he swallowed, he mouthed the word bitch as he realized Helen was not afraid of him.

She'd been afraid for ten years; from the time she was three years old until she was thirteen. The only reason it stopped was because her mother was found dead and she moved in with her mother's sister. She couldn't be shaken by the likes of Floyd.

Floyd finally gave up on his attempt and refocused his attention on Hazel and the Bishop, who were standing nearby. Helen told Sissy to go and join her brothers while she introduced herself to some of the folks attending the funeral.

She waited until Sissy become occupied with talking to her siblings before she sought out Floyd. When the time was right, she walked up to him and introduced herself as Helen, Sissy's stepsister.

Floyd was caught off guard but rebounded quickly. "Floyd, my name is Floyd," he said with his leering grin. "Soon to be Sissy's step-daddy. It's nice meeting you."

Helen pulled Floyd aside and out of hearing range of anyone who was paying attention to them. "My spineless father told me about you before he died," she said, even though she hadn't truly talked to him since she was thirteen. Helen stuck out her hand to shake his, but before Floyd could tough her hand Helen said, "I've always wanted to meet a piece of shit like you," and withdrew her hand before he could touch her.

Floyd stood there dumbfounded. Helen wasn't through with her whispered assault just yet. "I won't rest until your black ass is in jail for raping children or even better until your black ass is buried near your sick soul mate, my father." With that, she imitated his goofy grin and walked away.

She wasn't done introducing herself. Next, she walked up to the Bishop and Hazel, who were still walking around wearing their official 'I lost a loved one faces.'

"Hello, my name is Helen," she said. "You don't know me but I just brought your nine year old daughter back from the cemetery where you left her. I have no choice but to turn this incident in to Children and Youth Services on Monday, unless I'm allowed to visit her or talk to her at least once a week to assure myself that she's not being neglected."

Hazel and the Bishop stood there speechless. Helen wasn't going to hesitate to put herself in a position to put a stop to her sister's abuse.

"Do I know you?" asked Hazel. "You look familiar."

"I should look familiar, your husband was once accused of having my mother killed. I understand that you cleared him from suspicion by swearing he was with you — even though at the time you were just 13 and he was 49. It may be that I slightly resemble my father, God forbid. For years I've hated him because of the things he did to me when I was a child, plus most people believe he had someone kill my mother and make it look like rape. Of course you wouldn't know anything about any of that, would you?"

"Dat's crazy, I don't know you and I think you ought ta leave my baby and me alone."

"Oh, *now* she's your baby. An hour ago you didn't care where she was."

"Leave me and my baby alone."

"Young lady, just settle down," the Bishop interjected. "This is not the time or place for this discussion. Mrs. Williams has just lost her loving husband and—"

"Bullshit, Reverend. Her loving man is right over there drooling all over her nine year old daughter while you chase little boys."

"Young lady, you have to go, you're not welcome here. We will not put up with your accusations."

"Fine, I'm leaving, but I *will* check on Sissy. If need be, I'll try and get legal custody of her if I think she's being abused. In the mean time, I suggest you keep your stinkin' boyfriend away from her."

Helen walked over to Sissy on her way out of the church. "Hey, little sister. I'll be checkin' in on you and I'll never be far away if you need anything. You and me, okay? Don't be afraid."

"Yeah," Sissy said, "I'm not afraid, big sister."

Helen smiled at her once more and walked over to Floyd. "See ya, you piece of shit."

Floyd lifted up his head and grinned. "I know who you are now. I might have to do you like I did yo momma. I taught her some respect."

Helen was shocked by what Floyd had just said. *Did he know my mother? Of course he did. Floyd and her father were probably friends back then. Maybe he's the one who killed my mother.* That thought sent chills down her spine. Her outspokenness and courage might cause little Sissy and her to regret the confrontation with Floyd.

As she left the church, she walked through a rear gate and onto the pavement, heading toward her car. She felt like someone was looking at her and she quickly turned around to see who it was. There was no one there. She breathed a sigh of relief and quickly walked to the safety of her car.

Glancing up at a darkened room on the second floor of the church she wondered how many boys the Bishop had frightened into submission using the wrath of God as the tool of fear. As she looked back down at the gate she had just come through, she thought she saw a man, but as she looked closer at him, he had vanished.

Ozz found himself admiring her from afar. *Did she saw me?* he wondered. He was standing in the evening shadows of the open wrought iron gate and it had seemed like she looked back at him. The fragrance of her hair still lingered in the summer air. He watched as she turned again and looked back at the church that loomed behind him. He humbly raised his right hand in a vain attempt to get her attention. She stared for a second and then slowly turned and continued toward her car.

With her back to Ozz she paused as if she sensed that some one was watching. Quickly she looked back over her shoulder, only to find that there was no one there. Ozz raised his hand once more without the slightest response from Helen. Despite the boundaries that separated him from Helen, he admired her beyond belief. To Ozz, she was a perfect example of a beautiful and courageous woman.

For a brief second he thought he'd caught her eye. *Hello, precious woman,* he thought. *There is no way that she could see me, it just couldn't happen twice. I think, like many others, she sensed I was here. I wish she could see me. I wish I could talk to her. I wonder what it would be like to hold her close. If I were human, I would love her like no other.*

Helen was standing at her car door trying to locate her keys at the bottom of her purse. "Damn it, someone should invent keys that are easier to find," she said and chuckled to her self.

"Ah-ha, here you are," she said happily as she finally found the keys. She clicked the key fob and the interior lights to came on, revealing someone's reflection in the glass.

She was momentarily rigid, but quickly rebounded, opened the door, got in and slammed it shut. She immediately hit the lock door button and looked around, but there was no one there. She regained her composure and looked once more toward the gate. "What is wrong with me? I'm sitting here imagining something good could be at this church."

*I remember her now. She once cried out just as Sissy does now. Ironically, they both had the same abusive father,* thought Ozz. *She's not crying out now. Now she is something to behold, she's proud and protective, as I myself should be. She's a lot like her mother was, and I clearly remember what happened to her when she threatened to expose Floyd and the Bishop for what they had been doing to some of the children at the church. These people are evil hearted and only the Helen's of the world can put a stop to their sick acts.*

*She seems to have taken Sissy into her heart. I truly think she'll remove her from that circle of pedophiles. I've got to continue my efforts to intervene, though. I've got to help her in every way I can. Maybe she's strong enough. She certainly has the motives. The rapist of her stepsister, the murderer of her mother and now the threat on her own life. More than likely she can do more than I will ever be able to.*

# CHAPTER 20

It was 8:30 p.m., and just getting dark as Helen drove into her driveway. She sat in the car for a moment thinking about her day. *How did I find the courage to go to my father grave? He caused me so much grief and so many bad memories, I'm surprised at myself.* She'd been so sympathetic to Sissy and what the child must've gone through and probably was going through with Floyd. *Now I've gone and confronted the people that can ruin my safe and secure life.*

Why did I do that? she kept asking herself. She thought of what Floyd had said about teaching her mother to respect him. *Did he hurt my mother or was he just trying to scare me because of the threats I made about Sissy? Can I really help little Sissy?*

She knew it wasn't good to hate, even though it was warranted. The thought of what she said and did at her father's gravesite only proved that she was truly his daughter. *People like Henry, Floyd and the Bishop, who rape babies for pleasure and power, deserve to be hated. But that's what they expect. They expect to someday be exposed. They believe others will acknowledge them and say, 'I understand. I've done it too!' They believe that what they do is common and acceptable. This is where their sickness lies. The likes of Floyd may believe that it's not hate but jealousy that brings out my anger. He has that sly look on his face that says, 'You know you belong to me. This is truly where you want to be, under the wings of a man who molds children to believe that they are not victims. He's just like my father!*

*Then there's that Bishop, a leader of his congregation who teaches the importance of virginity being taken by sanctified men of great stature, like it says in the Bible. And then he gives these children to those horrid men and tells the child he or she is blessed to give up their virginity.*

"I was there", she said aloud. *I was there. He took away my sight. He taught me to think I was special to be his tool of pleasure. He taught me that it was God's wish. He also told me that Momma would be angry and disappointed if she knew, and that he would have to hurt her if she knew, because she would be jealous of the love he had for his special daughter. I am so filled with hate for those who place themselves in a void somewhere between good and evil. Their acts are truly the root of all evil!*"

PART THREE

# FLOYD, FLOYD: CHILD MOLESTER

# CHAPTER 21

Floyd asked the Bishop if he knew Helen, the girl that had confronted them at the church. "I'm not sure. She said she was Henry's daughter with his second wife. You know we knew her. Henry cultivated the young baby as his own until his wife found out and threatened to have all of us arrested for child abuse. I know you and Henry did the right thing. I guess we should've kept her little ass with us."

"What we gonna do 'bout her now?" Floyd asked.

"I don't think we need to do anything. Henry's dead and she doesn't have any idea what happen to her mother. All we know is she got her sassy ass raped and killed. Right?"

"Yeah, right, but I don't want her stirring up Sissy and her momma. That my family now and Sissy and her momma got a few more good years in 'em, if I keep 'em in line. You know it ain't gonna be the same witout Henry. I kinda liked sneakin' in when Henry went to work. Henry had dat young Sissy trained to just shut-up. He didn't mind me doing Hazel, but boy was he mad when he found out I had little Sissy goin' as much as he did. It just ain't gonna be the same takin' them young virgins witout Henry there tryin' to get a look. I just always pretended I didn't see him."

# CHAPTER 22

Weeks had gone by since Sissy's father's death and they'd been weeks without her being sexually molested by Floyd. It hadn't taken long for her to fit into this simple pattern. It seemed like the beginning of an ordinary life for the nine-year-old.

Floyd continued to come to her home on a nightly basis to spend time with Hazel and of course, get a free meal and occasional full night's stay. For the first couple of weeks, Sissy was uneasy knowing that Floyd was in the house while she was in bed trying to sleep. She was often awakened by the noises that could be heard through the thin walls that separated her room from her mother's.

In the years past, she always wondered why she could hear nearly every whisper coming from her parents' room, but they didn't seem to be able to hear Floyd's groans and grunts as he had his way with her after quietly sneaking into her room.

There were recent nights when she was awaken by the noises of Floyd apparently reaching his satisfaction and getting up to dress and leave for the night. He often paused for what seemed like an eternity in front of Sissy's bedroom door. She always found herself tense and filled with the fear that he would once again punish her for just being a child. It was worse now that he could have his way with her without repercussions from anyone. She just waited until she heard the back door close before she went to sleep.

On this night, after hearing the back door close, Floyd re-entered and slammed the door behind him. Sissy was wide-awake as he stomped loudly up the steps swearing as he reached the top landing. He punched her mother's door open and entered.

"What's wrong with you?" Hazel asked him.

"Don't play with me, bitch. Where's my god-damn money?" he said while snatching the covers off Hazel and throwing them to the floor. "Where's my motha-fuckin' money?"

"What you talkin' about, baby? I ain't seen no money."

"I said don't play wit me, bitch. Get up outta there and get my money."

Hazel jumped up immediately and began to look around on the floor while Floyd was still raving.

"You no good bitch," he said. "You think you can take somethin' from Floyd? I'll kill you!" he hollered, while smacking her on the side of her face with his full force. Hazel stumbled after he struck her and knocked down a small table. He struck her again as she tried to get to her feet.

"Where's my money? I ain't gonna ask you again," he said as he violently pushed her to the floor and onto her back. "Where is it?"

Hazel was dazed and couldn't get a word out as Floyd continued on his rampage.

"Leave my momma alone!" Sissy screamed as she entered the room and began to attack Floyd, swinging her little fist as hard as she could. Sissy fought Floyd like a child who had gone mad. She scratched, kicked and bit him in every way she could. Floyd tried to ignore her and stay focused on Hazel, who had gotten up and stepped between Floyd and Sissy.

"Wait! Wait!" Hazel said. "I don't have your money. Let's look for it. It must be here somewhere. Let's just look for it." During the scuffle with Sissy, Floyd's hat had fallen off and exposed his money. He'd forgotten he'd tucked it away in the rim. "There it is, right there in yo hat, where you put it. I told you I didn't have it."

Sissy was still swinging and clawing at Floyd until he finally looked down at her and shoved her to the floor. "Stop, Sissy! Just go to yo room. I'll handle dis," Hazel said, while helping Sissy up and pushing her out the door. "I tole you I didn't touch ya damn money."

"Shut up, bitch," Floyd said as he left the room and slammed the door behind him. Sissy listened as Floyd stormed down the steps and out the door. She had never known him to use the front door.

Sissy whimpered and quietly cried herself to sleep. Right before she dozed off, she wondered, *Where are my brothers? Why didn't they help Momma?* Then she remembered they were afraid of Floyd. *Plus, Momma told them many times not to come out of that back bedroom, no matter what they heard. They didn't even come out when momma and daddy fought violently. Those nights, he'd get exhausted and come climb into bed with me. No one ever seemed to hear my pleas.*

Sissy had been asleep for several hours when she felt someone's breath on her face, panting. She was frightened but opened her eyes and jerked back because found herself looking directly into Floyd's smiling face.

"You miss ole Floyd don't ya? Floyd gonna give you what ya need," he said while unzipping his dirty jumpsuit.

The courage that Sissy had displayed defending her mother had left her. Floyd stood before her in his frightful tormenting way and all she could do was wish that he would leave her alone. She wanted, like so many times before, to scream; but no one ever came to her aid so it wasn't worth the effort. She wanted to hit, kick and fight with all her might, but she was too afraid. He was so big and so mean. Sissy, as before, chose to hope he would be sympathetic; to hope he would realize she was only a child. *I just wish he would go and bother someone else, anyone else. Just leave me alone.*

Just as all the times before, he didn't care. He only wanted to torment her for the sake of his own sick desire. He wanted to have his own way, right under God's nose. "Please don't," she quietly pleaded, but Floyd continued his assault.

# CHAPTER 23

Ozz felt Sissy's distress. He began to move his heart toward an all out attack against Floyd. "Maybe this time I can intervene. Maybe this time will be his last."

"No!" came the voice of one of their senior angels. "We have determined that our interference with the acts of mankind can only lead to a ever-growing sense of frustration for the entire host of heavenly angels. Only God and man himself can counter the evil that lies here on earth, for there are thousands of Floyds. As we speak, the seeds of evil are growing within the hearts of many. They have refused to recognize the pleas of the innocent. Instead, these men and women have chosen the path of disruption. They play the part of selfish and evil fools, thinking God has abandoned these children.

"You, like the evil hearts of men, also have weakened enough to believe that God has abandoned his children. As strange as it seems, God has purposely given evil a place to dwell within the hearts of men," the senior angel said.

"But even little Sissy has the instincts to protect her own. Why is it that God has chosen to leave children at the mercy of humanity?" asked Ozz.

"Because God is God and only He can bring evil to its knees. God is the cure for those who have suffered. The assault is not upon the children; it is upon God himself. You and Chism must, from this point forward, leave the acts of evil to mankind." With that being his final word, the senior angel left their presence.

Chism took the words of the angel to heart and pledged to let God's way stand for right or wrong. Ozz kept his mind on the children, who he had watched suffer, and decided to make one more effort to help Sissy.

*Helen,* he thought to himself. *I must find a way to cause Helen to take up the fight for her sister and those like her.*

# CHAPTER 24

In a flash, Ozz found himself at Helen's side. He could see the sense of concern Helen had since her meeting with Sissy. *How can I make you see your sister's need for you to be in her life?* he wondered. *How can I make you and others like you stand up for the wellbeing of the children and uncloak the disguised pedophiles?*

Helen was filled with anger at the thought of men and women like Floyd. She would like nothing more than to expose the sick and evil pedophiles to expose for all to see, so they could no longer conducted their evil behind of the closed door of secrecy.

She began to feel a driving need to protect her long lost sister. "I think," she said to herself, "I will go by Sissy's school. Maybe I'll see her. Maybe I'll get a chance to talk to her."

*Yes,* thought Ozz. *Yes, yes, yes!*

# CHAPTER 25

Something continued to draw Helen to the elementary school on South Street. Finally she took off early from work and drove to within a block of the school. She got out of her car and walked to the side entrance of Franklin Elementary, just as the children began to walk out of the front door.

Helen searched the crowd of children hoping to find Sissy. Within a few moments, the exodus of children began to thin out to just a trickle. *I guess I must've missed her in the crowd.* Disappointed, she began to walk back to her car. *Maybe she didn't come to school today. Maybe she's sick or maybe those idiots have just taken her out of school. I'll keep trying, until I at least see her from afar.*

"Hello, big sister." Helen snapped out of her thoughts at the sounds of Sissy's voice. "Are you lost or something?"

"No- no I'm not lost. I was just walking along... Fancy meeting you here, little sister. It seems like we meet in the strangest places. I'm so glad to see you. I've been thinking about you a lot. How about I walk you home?" Helen asked.

"Okay, I live down there," she said pointing toward her home.

"Better yet, lets sit here and talk first. Is that all right or do you think you'll get into trouble?"

"No, I won't get in trouble. I always take a long time to walk home. Sometimes, I sit and watch the high school kids walk by just for something to do."

"So, little sister, how are you? I've missed you. I've been wondering if you're all right."

Sissy just looked up at Helen like she was bursting at the seams with a thousand stories about herself. *I wish I could ask her to help me find a way be happy. A hug would be nice, too,* she thought wistfully. She hunched her shoulders and said, "I'm all right."

Helen felt a compassionate urge to hug her little sister and without a word she bent over toward Sissy and opened her arms. "Come here and give me a hug. I need it so bad."

Sissy walked into the open arms of her big sister and was enveloped in the warmth and caring in her touch. The two of them sat quietly for a while before Sissy decided to talk.

"Do you think I'm a good girl?" Sissy asked.

"I know you're nothing but the best."

Sissy paused for a few moments, looking toward her home. "I don't like going home."

"Why not?"

"Because its always crazy there. Everyone's afraid of Floyd. He hits my brothers on the head real hard. They run when he comes in."

"Are you scared?"

"Kinda ... I pretend he's gone away a lot and that makes me feel happy. But, he always comes back."

"Does he hit you?"

"No, he doesn't hit me ... but he hit my momma before."

"If he hits you, I'm gonna punch him right in his nose!" Helen said, and they both laughed at her punching gesture and scrunched up face.

They sat quietly again, just looking around at the straggling students who walked by.

"Do you have to leave soon?" Sissy asked.

"No, I'm not leaving until you want me to."

"I never want you to."

"Then I'm never going to leave, except sometimes I have to go home and eat and brush my teeth, and maybe sleep a little. You know ... things like that," Helen said bringing another smile to Sissy's face. "What if I told you that when I was a little girl I was exactly like you? I thought a lot of the other kids didn't like me. Do you feel that way sometimes? I mean, that other kids think you're different from them or that you think you're different because you have bad people in your house?"

"Yeah."

"I used to cry at night because my dad wouldn't leave me alone. He always hugged, kissed and touched me where I didn't want to be touched. Sometimes I wanted to puke, but I was afraid he would get angry and do something worse. I remember thinking that no matter how bad I felt he could always make it worse. I was afraid of what worse might be.

Now that I'm older, I realize that it couldn't have gotten worse because there was nothing worse than what I was living through. I hope I'm not confusing you, little sister. I just want you to know that things do get better. Try not to be afraid. In fact, I'm going to give you my phone number so you can call me when you want to talk."

"Are you going now?" asked Sissy.

"No, little sister. Not yet. I wish I could take you home with me," Helen said.

"Me too," Sissy said. "I wish you could be with me, in my room at night. Its scary, and sometimes I think someone is trying to get me when I'm sleep. I bet no one would try and get in my room if you were there."

"No, they wouldn't. We'd punch 'em. Right? Here's my phone number, and I want you to call me every chance you get. I'll come down here as often as I can so you and I can talk. Okay?"

"Okay. Are you leaving now?" Sissy asked sadly.

As the two of them stood up, a truck horn blew. They stopped talking and looked to see who was trying to get their attention. It was Floyd. "What you doin' talkin' to my baby? You jus a stranger. You ain't got no business keepin' her from comin' home. You get on home, Sissy. I'm gonna tell yo momma you talkin' to strangers," he said.

"Number one, she's *not* your baby. Number two, I'm not a stranger; I'm her sister. Number three, I'm going to walk her home whether you like it or not," Helen said.

Floyd stared at Sissy, his anger clear, as he stomped on the gas and sped down the street.

"Come on, little sister. I'm walking you all the way home."

"No!" Sissy responded adamantly. "He's gonna hurt Momma and me if you make him mad. He's gonna hurt us," she repeated.

"No, he's not going to hurt anybody or he'll go to jail where he belongs." As they walk up the concrete front steps of her house, Sissy began to act uneasy. "Come on, little sister. I'm with you, don't be afraid."

"He's gonna hurt me."

Helen stopped and faced Sissy. "Has he ever hit you, Sissy?"

Sissy didn't answer.

"Has he ever hit you?" she asked again.

"No, but he hurts me and hits my momma sometimes. I don't want you to go in."

"Don't you worry, he's not going to do anything. He's just a coward. I'm going to talk to your mother." Helen knocked on the door. There was no answer. She knocked again and again still no one came. She turned the knob and the door sprung open. "Hello, is anyone home?"

"Yeah, three somebody here and it's me," a voice said. "Come on in here."

Helen thought she recognized Floyd's voice. All the window curtains were drawn, making the house dark even though the sun was still shining brightly outside. Helen felt a chill of fear run down her spine. "Where's Mrs. Williams?" she asked. There was no answer. As courageous as Helen wanted to be, she wasn't brave enough to walk further into the room.

"Come on in. Hazel's in here wit me," the voice calmly said. Helen edged in a little further keeping the open front door with Sissy standing on the threshold, completely in sight. She peeked around the corner leading into the living room. "Mrs. Williams, I need to talk to you about Sissy. Can you come out here, please, or turn on the lights so I can see you?" There was no response. Helen heard the back door slam shut, then heard someone turn the lock.

"I'm not afraid of you, Floyd. I'm not a small child you can frighten and abuse. Mrs. Williams, if you don't speak up I'm going to take Sissy and leave. Mrs. Williams, please answer me."

Suddenly she heard Sissy say, "No!" as the front door was slammed shut from the inside. "Leave me alone!" Sissy screamed. Helen heard the lock turn as Sissy continued to scream. "Get off of me! I hate you! Get ... off ... me!" Sissy screamed and ran to Helen.

"Okay, little sister. I've got you. We're safe now. He'd better not even think of putting his hands on you!" Helen loudly said. "What kind of man are you that you'd frighten a child like this?"

Out of the dark, a sudden and powerful blow struck the side of Helen's face causing her to lose consciousness and slump to the floor.

"No! No! No! No! No!" Sissy screamed.

"Leave us alone!" Sissy screamed and was then slung violently against the stairs and knocked unconscious.

As Helen began to regain her senses, she tried to stand but a forceful hand slapped hard against her chest and grabbed her by her bra. She was then slung into the living room and ended up on to the floor.

With two hard yanks, her shirt and bra were ripped from her upper body. Half-dazed she continued to try to get up. There were no words, just Helen's heavy panting as she tried to fight off her unknown assailant. The room was spinning around her as she stumbled backward and crashed into an end table, flattening it to the floor with her weight. Again she pushed herself and quickly got to her feet, she leaned against the wall and swung her fists in front of her in an attempt to hold off whoever was attacking her.

The huge hand grabbed her by the front of her pants and swung her from right to left, banging her against the walls. A hand tucked deep between her lower belly and the buckle of her belt tugged violently, pulling her back down to the floor on her knees. Again, there was a slight pause, as if her attacker had vanished.

Her strength was depleted and she couldn't get to her feet. Suddenly she was yanked by her hair and then lifted off the floor and slammed down hard enough to nearly knock her unconscious again. Helen twisted herself toward the window, where a crack of light had made its way into the room. With all her might she reached out and pulled down the curtains, letting in a burst of sunlight that seemed to explode into the room.

In the now brightly lit room, she fought desperately to get free from the dusty curtains she'd pulled down on herself. Exhausted, Helen finally got the last curtain off her head. Every breath she took seemed to set her lungs on fire. The dust and curtain fibers floated in the sunlight and a sudden stillness brought on a feeling of peace.

She coughed as she rolled to her knees and began to crawl toward the foyer where Sissy lay unconscious. Helen put her head on Sissy's shoulder just as Sissy began to stir. Together they sat up with their backs against the staircase wall so they could clearly see into the living room.

The room was trashed. At the base of the front window the sunlight now sparkled against everything that was reflective. Even the dust, which scurried through the air, seemed to sparkle as if the whole incident had never happened. No one else was there. There was no Floyd, either. There was no one here but Helen and Sissy, who were looking around the room fearfully wondering what would happen next.

*Did Floyd leave the room while I fought with drapes?* Helen wondered. *I've never experienced such a powerful force in my life. The hand that grabbed me was much larger than I thought possible. At one point, it seemed to span the entire front of my body. Was it just my imagination or should I admit I never actually saw Floyd? Has Sissy ever gone through this type of violent encounter before?*

She cleared her throat and asked Sissy, "Are you all right?"

Sissy didn't answer. She looked up with tears flowing down her face and hugged Helen tight. Helen wrapped her arms around the child and tried to comfort her.

# CHAPTER 26

"You two are lucky," said the Washington detective. "You must've walked in on a burglar. There is some question as to how or why both the front and back doors are bolted from inside, but, uh, since neither of you actually saw the burglar I guess he's gotten away with it this time. We'll get him. Don't worry about that. They always keep at it until we catch 'em and put 'em away."

"This wasn't a burglar, sir," said Helen. "This was an attempted rape. Why don't you ask Floyd where he was?"

"Miss, you said you didn't see anyone. You can't just accuse a man of committing a crime simply because you don't like him."

"But I know it was him and I think he has abused the young girl that lives here."

"Hold it now, you're getting carried away. That's enough of these unfounded accusations," the police officer said.

Helen realized just how close she'd come to being raped. She could only imagine what Sissy must've been going through if her suspicions were correct. She was almost positive that Floyd was not only a potential rapist, but also an active pedophile with Sissy as his primary victim. The big question remained, what exactly could she do to get Sissy out of harm's way.

The police were convinced that the intruder was a burglar and that Helen had just been in the way causing the burglar to fight his way out. In truth, they couldn't be more wrong. Someone, or something, had attacked Helen and Sissy with the intention of doing harm. Helen was sure of it.

When the police left, Helen made the decision to speak kindly to Sissy's mother. *Maybe, just maybe if I approach Hazel properly she'll understand she has to do something for the sake of her daughter.*

"Mrs. Williams, I guess you're wondering how I got here. Maybe you're even wondering what really happened."

"No, I know what happen. You and Sissy tore up my house and it don't have nothin' to do with Floyd 'cause he was with me and the boys."

"Are you serious? You believe that I would just come into your house and tear it up without rhyme or reason?"

"Yeah, 'cause you had reason. You hate me 'cause I took your daddy away from yo momma 'fore she die. Now you don't want to see me wit Floyd. I know Sissy don't like Floyd 'cause she always makes up stuff 'bout him. I'll tell you somethin', missy, Floyd a good man. I ain't gonna let you or Sissy mess up me an my man."

"But, he's hurt your daughter. Sissy has told you that herself."

"He ain't did no such thing. Sometime he show her 'bout what a young girl should know, so she don't have ta learn it from the streets. That good for Sissy 'cause she need to be ready for life."

"What are you talking about? She's just a child. You can't possibly believe those stupid things he and my daddy told you about their way of showing love. He did it to me, and my guess is he did it to Sissy, too. You can't possibly believe these men are doing something that benefits your child. Wait. Listen, Mrs. Williams, I don't want to upset you. I just want to be a part of my sister's life. I'll pay for the damages, if you'll just let me spend some time with Sissy. Please, Mrs. Williams, it will be good for both of us."

By now Floyd had come in and caught the tail end of the conversation. "Naw," Floyd said, "we don't need nobody tryin' ta poison Lil Sissy 'bout how we do. You need ta get out."

"I was talking to Mrs. Williams, not you."

"What you mean, bitch? I done tole ya ta get out!" Floyd shouted, while pushing Helen's shoulder."

"Mrs. Williams, look at your daughter. She's scared to death of this man. There's no telling what he's done to her. Let's do this. Floyd, if you'll just let me talk to my sister on the phone sometimes, I'll promise not to bother you. If you say no, I swear I'll use every means available to me to persuade Children's Services to examine Sissy for sexual abuse. I will not rest until I'm sure she's not neglected."

"Naw," Floyd said, "I want you outta dis house and away from us 'cause you ain't no damn good."

"Please, Mrs. Williams. Think about Sissy for once in your life."

"I'll think about it, but right now you need to go," Hazel said.

Helen walked toward the front door and turned once more to say goodbye to Sissy, who had been sitting quietly during their heated conversation.

"Good-bye, little sister" Helen said.

"Bye" Sissy said glumly.

"Get on out, and don't come back. Next time somebody might get ya for real," Floyd said with his typical nasty grin.

Helen walked the nearly four-block trek to her car, fuming. She had to get Sissy away from that horrible man.

# CHAPTER 27

As Helen drove east on North Avenue, she the undeniable urge to look in her rear view mirror. She looked and noticed that about two blocks behind her was a menacing looking pick-up truck. To see if it was following her, she pulled over to the curb — so did the truck. She pulled out onto North again and made a right turn onto Oakwood, the truck was right behind her. She drove to Arlington and took a left onto Penn Avenue — the truck was still following at about the same distance. Again, she pulled to the curb and watched as the truck also parked and turned its lights off.

This has not been one my days, and now someone's following me," she said to herself. She sat watching the truck. It looked like a man sitting behind the wheel smoking a cigarette. Helen wasn't afraid yet, but she was contemplating just what she should do next.

*I can't just drive home and let whoever that is find out where I live — especially since I'm home alone tonight,* she thought. *I can't just sit here, either.* Two young black men were walking on the sidewalk toward her car, so she rolled down her window and said, "Excuse me. Can you help me? There's a man in that pick-up truck about a half of block behind me. He's been following me and I'm afraid he means to hurt me. Can you ask him why he's following me?"

"Are you sure he's been following you?" one of the men asked.

"Yes — he's been behind me every time I turn, and when I parked, so did he. I think he may be following me so he can rob me when I get out of my car. I don't know what to do."

"We'll handle it, sister. When he pulls off you should head the other way," the man said.

She watched in the rear view mirror as the two men walked up to the pick-up. One of them crossed in front of the truck and approached the driver. "Hey, man, why you messin' with the sister?"

"Mind your own business, boy," said the driver of the truck.

"How'd you like it if I pull you out of that truck and whip your ass. Would that be my business, nigga?"

"I think you betta beat it fore you get hurt, boy," the man in the truck threatened, while showing him is pistol.

"Hey, you got it man," he said as both of the young men raised their hands and backed away from the truck.

"You did da right thing 'cause I'd blow yo brains out just for the hell of it," the driver said as he started his vehicle and put it in gear.

Helen watched as the truck pulled forward toward her at a high rate of speed. The two strangers looked on, helpless. Just before the truck hit her car, it made a sharp U-turn and sped back down Penn Avenue. Helen continued to watch until the truck's taillights were nearly out of sight.

She sighed in relief and waved to the two men as a gesture of thanks. She quickly made her way home, looking at her rear view mirror often. She was shaken but she had no intention of giving up on her little sister. *This is just the beginning,* she thought. *God willing, somehow I'm going to get my sister away from those sick evil people. I will not let her go it alone, no matter what it takes.*

# CHAPTER 28

A loud banging on his back door woke Bishop Jones. "I hope this is a friendly visit," he said as he made his way to the door. "Who is it?" he said without opening the door.

"Its me, Floyd. Let me in, Rev. We need to talk."

The Bishop quickly unlatched the door and let Floyd in. "What're you doing out so late?"

"We gotta talk. That damn woman that was at Henry's funeral was at da house today wit Sissy. I think she knows 'bout what we did to her momma."

"What are you talking about? There's no way she knows anything. If she does, she's going to end up with her momma."

"I'm tellin' you, Rev, she know. Ain't no tellin' what else she know. Ya think she remembers what we did to her?"

"No, she can't remember or she would've told someone long ago. Most of these children think they did something wrong because they think they played apart in our little sex rituals. They're just as ashamed as we are fulfilled. Anyway, you know they like it, Floyd. All we have to do is keep her away from all of the children we've indoctrinated. No one's going to believe Sissy Williams. Plus who is she going to tell? Most of the teachers and policemen around here are gettin' more than us. Anyway, I thought you and Hazel had Sissy under control."

"She's startin' ta get older now. I keep tellin' her, I ain't gonna tell nobody what she been doin' to me, but I think dat Helen's tellin' her she ain't done nothin' wrong. You know dat's when we got trouble, when they start talkin' to people."

"Well, you've got to make her think she's a nasty dog. You know how to do it, Floyd. You can't enjoy the young virgin fruits if you can't make convince them they're causing it to happen. Sissy's getting to an age where she needs to be convinced that she's been doing you of her own free will. If we can't plant that guilt, she's going to talk. We can't have CYS snooping around our church's school rooms."

"What we gonna do 'bout Helen?"

"F-her, she's probably feeling guilty about all the screwing she did with her daddy. If she talks, she tells on herself. You know that's the last thing they want is for someone to know they've been sexually active since they were four or five years old. They're embarrassed to talk to anyone they think might see them as used up sex children. Don't worry that much about Helen. If she goes too far and starts stirring up trouble, do the same thing you done to her mother."

"Rev, ain't you got some new young stuff at da church I can get wit?"

"No, Floyd. That's your problem. You want too many. It's not as easy to break today's kids in like it used to be. These parents are starting to watch their children since all these talk shows are bringing them out of the closet, so to speak. We've got to be careful. There are a lot of important men that count on our church to provide them with the pleasures of virgin child sex. They can't stop. They're like junkies. Nothing satisfies like the cry of a young child."

"Stop it, Rev! You makin' me horny wit dat talk."

"Well, you need to get un-horny and take care of business. None of these folks that come to the church want any kind of publicity — they've got the money to keep it quiet and you don't. So, get out, 'cause I'm sleepy and I've got clients to meet tomorrow.

"Dat Helen said somebody try to rape her ole ass down at the house today. The police was there."

"You didn't tell me that. Who was it? Do you know?"

"Naw, wasn't nobody there. Da police said it prob'ly a burglar."

"Well, I'm going to pray on it. A lot has happened in that house and little Sissy is usually at the center of it. Sometimes, I think she wasn't a good choice. She always seemed to be special, but you and her father just had to make her a sex child."

"There you go with dat shit 'bout Sissy bein' good. She ain't no different than any of da otha young virgins."

"Yes, but I get a feeling sometimes that the devil himself rejoices at the abuse of the good seeds. Every once in a while, I've read and heard that the devil flaunts his victories over a seed of God. That's nothing to mess with. The devil can be a powerful spirit. Especially when he's bold enough to taunt God himself.

"That Sissy child never should've been chosen for a sex virgin. You're never going to break her spirit. She's just too proud and too determined. I've always had the feeling that God sometimes gives us enough line to choke ourselves. You know time is always on His side. Sooner or later He will claim His own and we'll have hell to pay.

"Oh, well. Let's enjoy it while we can. Now get out. I've got to get some rest. Plus I've got a handsome little fellow back in the room that nobody wants but me. Get goin'!"

# CHAPTER 29

Floyd got back to Sissy's house a little after 3 a.m. He came in the back door and slammed it shut behind him as hard as he could. This had always been Floyd's way of instilling fear the moment he crossed the threshold.

He stomped up the steps, waking Sissy before he reached the top. She peaked from her covers as he made his usual pause to look in at her doorway. Floyd mumbled a few words Sissy couldn't quite make out and continued on to Hazel's room.

"Hazel, wake yo ass up! Dis is the last time I gonna tell you. Don't let nobody talk to Sissy. Ain't no tellin' what she done told dem woman. I want her to keep our business right here at home. If she don't I'll start whippin' yo ass just like Henry used to do. You hear me? I mean dat!"

# CHAPTER 30

Over the next few weeks, Helen worked hard at her landscaping company trying to keep worries about her sister from overwhelming her. The memories of her own childhood hung heavy in her heart to the point that it began to show in her day-to-day life. She would frequently stare at nothing, then bow her head and sigh.

Her frustration and helplessness tore at her until she knew she had to talk to someone. *I needed to be somebody she could trust who would understand what she and Sissy had gone through. It seems like there's nowhere to turn for a woman who has lived through sexual torment by her own father. What man would understand? What friend would be capable of comprehending the endless nightmares? What woman would sympathize with another who has kept this type of secret for so long? How could I ever begin? Would I say, "My daddy had his way with me, sexually, many times?"*

Yet, she found within herself an endless desire to tell someone about what ripped away all of her childhood happiness. She even fantasized about how the conversation would go,

*"I'd like to tell you about my daddy. He raped me almost every day with what he called love and affection. My daddy convinced me, at four years old, that sex was his special pleasure and only I could make him happy. If daddy wasn't happy, there was a house filled with anger and the screaming and abuse of my mother. But, when his baby pacified him, everything was quiet and calm."*

She'd never quite found the answers to the questions she'd been asking herself since she was four: What kind of daddy is this? What did I do to deserve the pain he inflicted? Why was it me?

What really bothered her was the fact that her same daddy, now dead and buried, had inflicted the very same misery on Sissy. *Now Sissy has to try to make sense of these cards life has dealt to her — just like me. She's got no one to talk to about it — just like me. Now, she has it worse than I did because she's living with the likes of Floyd, who has probably taken over where her father had left off.*

Helen had convinced herself long ago that she could recognize a child molester the moment he or she walked into a room. Floyd was different from any man she'd ever encountered. He didn't use the typical sweet talk of the traditional pedophile. He didn't approach with the warm, "trust me" attitude or holy disguise, or even the pretense of liking to play with children.

No, Floyd was different. He was cold and projected cruelty and harshness. *His kind must do it for a different reason, or this man is truly evil. He obviously finds sexual pleasure in a way that's beyond being a pedophile. This man's orgasm is connected to Satan's penis. When he reaches his pleasure, Satan is in ecstasy. This man is evil and he has my little sister in his control.*

"What's wrong, Helen?" the a kind voice of Jason, a fellow contractor, asked. Jason was a big man of about thirty-five, who stood more than six feet tall. He was the father of three daughters. "Anything you'd like to talk about?"

"No, I was just day dreaming."

"Well, you looked like you were in pain. You know we've got to stick together. There aren't many black contractors around Washington. If this is getting to you, let's talk about it. Maybe it's not as bad as you think."

"No, its not that. This is only a job and it's only money. I can handle that. No, this is something personal."

"Oh, hey, I'm sorry. I didn't mean to pry. I thought it might've had something to do with this contract."

"It's okay. I'm glad you're concerned about me. But, really … I'm okay. I just have to think some things through."

"Well, if its money, I've always got at least a hundred dollars you can have," Jason said with a smile.

"I'll remember that. By the way, when are you going to finish this job? You've been up here longer than me."

"Hey, I don't want to think about it. I keep saying two more weeks at least once a month. We'll get it done, eventually."

Helen was nearly finished with the $60,000 landscaping job. Her work wasn't an issue, but she just couldn't stop thinking about Sissy. Her new business success was only satisfying to the bill collectors and retail stores she frequented. Those she met saw a young, successful, pretty woman who exuded confidence and business savvy. On the inside, though, she sometimes felt like the insecure, abused little girl.

Three weeks had passed since Helen had last seen Sissy. She'd stopped by the schoolyard a few times, but she hadn't seen her. Today, she'd made up her mind to find her, even if she had to go back to Sissy's home and deal with Floyd again.

She'd been standing at the front gate of the school for more than twenty minutes when Sissy came up from behind her and said, "Hello, big sister."

Helen turned and bent down to hug Sissy with all her might. "I'm so glad to see you," Helen said as she pulled back and looked at her sister. Then she gave her another warm hug. "You're a sight for sore eyes. I've missed you so much."

"I missed you, too," said Sissy.

Helen took Sissy's hand and said, "Let's take a walk. Okay?"

"Okay, but I've got to get home before my momma or she'll punish me."

"I'll tell you what. Let's go to the playground on the other side of the school. We can talk there."

"Okay."

While they walked, Helen kept repeating how much she missed Sissy. "I've come by the school a couple of times but I guess you'd already gone home or maybe you wasn't at school those days. I don't know."

"Well, I always go out the doors on the other side, near my homeroom class. I guess I didn't see you."

"Oh, silly me. I never thought that maybe you left from one of the other doors," Helen said as she smacked her own forehead. "Duh!"

The two sisters found their way to the playground swings and sat side by side.

"Did I get you into trouble a few weeks ago when I was at your house?" Helen asked with more serious facial expression.

"Kinda," Sissy answered.

"What happened?"

"I had to clean the house and wash clothes everyday, and I'm not allowed to talk to my brothers or play with them. I miss playing school. I like to be the teacher 'cause I'm the smartest."

"Did you get a beating?"

"I don't know," Sissy said and hunched her shoulders.

"What do you mean, you don't know? Did Floyd lay his hands on you?"

"I don't know."

"Please tell me, Sissy. I won't say anything to anyone. Did he touch you?"

Sissy bowed her head and sat on the swing looking at the ground.

"Are you afraid of him, little sister?"

Sissy sadly nodded her head yes.

"Has he ever touched you ... I mean touched you where he has no business touching you?"

Sissy didn't answer. "I got two A's today. One in math and one in spelling."

"That's my girl ... give me a high five," Helen said while holding her hand out for Sissy to slap.

"I'm the smartest kid in my class. My teacher says I'm going to be a doctor when I grow up. If I did that, I'd be making people well," Sissy said.

"Have you ever visited a doctor's office?" Helen asked.

Sissy shook her head no.

"I have a friend that's a doctor. Would you like to go to his office one day?"

"Yeah."

"You know, little sister, I'm not afraid of Floyd. He's a big strong man but he only scares little children like you ... and maybe sometimes women like me. But, we don't have to be so frightened that we can't talk to each other. Let's talk. Okay? Me first. See this scar?" Helen said showing Sissy a childhood scar on the back of her lower leg.

"My father, excuse me, our father gave me this scar for telling my mother he put his hands between my legs. The buckle of his belt cut my leg and blood went everywhere. I think it was on my fifth birthday. My mother stood up to him and told him if he ever touched me again she would turn him into the police.

"Then one day not long after that, we were alone and he touched me again. He held me down and put his nasty self all over me. When he was done, he told me that if I told anyone he would take my cousin Sue and throw her into the river! Then he promised that it would never happen again unless I wanted it to.

"I hated him because he hurt me and he lied. He did it again and again until my mother caught him and called the police. Not long after that, while daddy was in jail, someone strangled my mother during a robbery. After that, I went to live with my aunt in Alexandria. I had a really happy life there.

"My mother must've been fooled into marriage, because our father was never nice to her. He beat her all the time, but for my sake, I think she tried to make it work.

"For years I actually thought he would throw Sue into the river, so I just didn't tell. I thought it was better for me to suffer than for my cousin to drown." Helen paused and looked at Sissy and said, "Sister, just as I told you before, everybody's not like our father was. There are good people who would never harm a child or anyone else. People like our dad rely on us to not tell the good people who would put a stop to their cruelty. They do it with threats to our loved ones and trickery like making us believe that we're the ones who initiate their deplorable acts.

"Some of them may even cry like our daddy did with me; making me think he was so sorry and scared that the police would put both of us in jail and we would never see my mother again. I believed him. He was a sick man and now I'm sure God has made him pay."

Again Helen paused and waited for Sissy to respond in some way. Sissy planted her feet on the ground, holding the seat of the swing behind her. She was still looking at her own feet. "I'm scared some times," Sissy said. "Sometimes, I think that Floyd will pull my brothers' nose and ears completely off. Sometimes, he pulls their ears and dares them to cry, and sometimes he holds them down and puts his knuckles on the top of their heads and rubs until they cry. Then, then he laughs and calls them fagots. He's so mean," Sissy said.

"Has he ever touched you, little sister?"

Sissy began to cry. With tears streaming down both of her cheeks, she looked up at Helen and said, "Please, big sister, don't make me tell. He will kill us. I know he will. It's just me he's bothering, and I'll do what he says. I just don't want him to kill us." Sissy snapped her head back down as if she realized she'd said too much and Floyd could hear every word she said.

"He's going to hurt me now. He's going to hurt all of us. He knows what I say. He always knows." She began to look around, up and down the street and even into the trees, sure that somehow Floyd had heard. "He heard me, big sister. I know he heard me." After that, Sissy wouldn't talk anymore.

Helen had no choice but to let Sissy go home alone. She watched as her poor little sister nervously walked away, occasionally looking back at Helen and modestly waving good-bye each time.

Helen slowly walked in the same direction as Sissy, wishing she could call her back and take her home with her. Just as Sissy reached the top of her porch steps, Floyd's truck pulled around the corner.

Helen impulsively ducked down behind a parked car. That familiar chill of fear ran down her spine. *I can't be afraid,* she thought. *I just can't be.* She peered over the hood of the parked car to find Floyd looking directly back at her. Quickly she ducked back down hoping he hadn't seen her. Again, she slowly looked to see if Floyd was still there. This time he was walking toward her. She ducked again, this time she had both knees on the ground.

*Oh, my God. He knows I'm here. I've got to be brave. Maybe he didn't see me.* She held her breath and waited for a few moments, hoping he would go away. Helen's breathing sounded like it was being amplified a hundred times louder than usual. She began to shake in fear. *I've got to be brave. I've got to get up and walk like the brave woman that I am.*

"Hey, bitch. What you doin' on yo knees? You lookin' for somethin' to suck?"

"You'd better leave me alone, Floyd. I'm not afraid of you," Helen said as she tried to stand up. Her legs had weakened and shook uncontrollably.

"You sure *look* scared, bitch. I thought I told you not to come round here messin' wit Sissy. I oughta just take my dick out and piss on ya. Look at ya shakin' like a leaf. Get on outta here. I'll deal wit you later. I'll do you just like yo daddy used to. I'm gonna hear you squeal like yo momma did when I pushed it in her back side with a wire around her neck."

"You son of a bitch!" Helen screamed and went berserk. She struck at him with all of her might, but Floyd sidestepped her and pushed her to the ground.

"Go head now, bitch, an get gone 'fore you get hurt."

Helen got up and continued to try to hit Floyd. Again he dodged and shoved her to the ground. "You a crazy hoe ain't you? Yo little sista is jus right. You old."

Again Helen got up and attacked him, swinging wildly and fighting in every way she could. This time Floyd struck her on the left side of her head and she thought her eardrum had exploded as she hit the ground again.

Helen got back up on her feet only to see Floyd's was nearly half a block away, heading for Sissy's house. Defeated and half-dazed, she walked back to her and rested her head on the steering wheel.

"God," she said, "please help us." Then, she cried like a child.

Beep! Beep! She heard a horn blow right next to her. She looked up and into Floyd's grinning face as he rolled down his window.

Her heart nearly came to a stop. *It's not over. He's going to kill me!* she thought. She hurriedly fumbled with her keys trying to get them into the ignition. "Come on! Come on! Come on!" she said, as the car started and she slammed it into gear. Within a second, she could see Floyd in her rear view mirror. He was standing next to his truck, looking at her retreating car. An oncoming car, which she nearly struck as she ran a stop sign, honked angrily at her. She was heading home. She did exactly what she said she would never do — abandon Sissy again.

Helen pulled into her driveway and just like before, sat and took in several deep breaths of air. It felt good to be in the safety of her own driveway in front of her own home. She pulled down the visor and flipped up the lighted mirror. The side of her face was bruised worse than when she'd had the encounter inside Sissy's house.

She took one more look at her face and flipped the mirror back up into position. With a deep breath, she pulled the door lever to exit the car. The door opened a little more than a foot before it made a thud sound of hitting against something. She pushed against the door a little harder and realized the door was pushing back. She couldn't see anything outside that could be blocking the door, so she pushed once more as hard as she could.

The door was pushed back again and this time it slammed shut, causing the interior light to turn off. Suddenly the Floyd's familiar frightening face came into view. "So, dis is where you live?" he said through the closed window.

Helen panicked and slammed her hand down onto the door lock. Floyd put his hands above the car door and pushed, making the car rock back and forth. Helen laid on the horn, trying to get someone's attention.

Floyd bent his head down and cupped his hands so he could see clearly inside. "Dis is yo last warning. Stay away from Sissy or I'll make it my business to teach you the lesson of your life. I mean it!" Floyd slammed his foot against her car door and walked confidently down the driveway.

Helen sat there, petrified. She had never known such fear.

# CHAPTER 31

A few days later at the construction site, Jason commented, "Look at you. Something really must've gotten to you. You look like you've lost your best friend."

"No, it's worse than that. Do you remember I told you that I met my nine-year-old stepsister at my father's funeral?"

"Yeah."

"Well, I've discovered that my father and his long-time friend, Floyd, had been sexually molesting her since she was four years old. She can't remember the first time. Not only that, but recently, during one of my run-ins with they guy who lives with them now, Floyd, he made it clear that he played a major part in the murder of my mother.

"Why is it that men like him and my father seem to get away with raping children and no one seems to care? At least it seems like no one ever does anything about it. They just go on with their lives, smiling at the neighbors and laughing with their friends like it's normal. This man has actually admitted to me that he enjoyed watching my mother take her last dying breath, as she begged him for mercy."

Helen paused for a moment and tried to hold back the tears that came to her eyes at the frustration she felt. "I just can't understand how God can let these men live."

"Listen, my friend," Jason said, "you can't let these things get to you. Trying to understand how sick people justify their acts can cause you a lot of misery — especially when it hits home. There are a lot of men who would love to avenge the lives of the women and children who have died or are seriously hurt at the hands of men who were supposed to be loving and caring."

"I know," Helen said. "But that doesn't fix the problem. They just continue to ambush helpless children at night and pretend to be good men around their daytime buddies. ... Will you do me a favor?" Helen asked.

"You know it," Jason answered.

"Come with me and meet my little sister. It won't take long. Maybe you'll see in her what I do. She's much more than just another nine-year-old. She's smart and charming beneath her shyness, and she's got an aura of innocence that can make you feel guilty of neglect."

"I'll go with you anywhere in a heartbeat. When are we going?" Jason asked in a serious tone.

"Let's go now. She'll be getting out of school in about a half an hour."

"This is as good a time as any."

As they drove from Oakland toward Homewood, Jason confided in Helen about the incident that resulted in the death of his own nine-year-old daughter. "I have harbored a constant pain of loss. I don't believe that I'll ever forgive myself for not being there for my daughter when that sick rapist killed her."

"Oh, Jason, I'm so sorry. I didn't know. Maybe we shouldn't go. I didn't realize you'd experienced such a tragedy. I wouldn't dare stir up those bad memories for you."

"No, it's all right. I think maybe its time for me to talk about it. It's just that it makes me so angry, even now. I'd do anything to have been there to protect my child. Now I just hurt until I actually tire myself out with hate."

"Do you want to tell me about it? You're always there for me when I'm lost in frustration, and I'd like to be there for you. Who knows, maybe I'll be able to lift some of your burden like you've lifted mine. Sometimes, just hearing yourself talk brings on a different level of understanding."

"Yes, we can talk about it. Maybe you're right. Maybe it wouldn't destroy my insides quite so much if I talk about it. My daughter lived up in Johnstown with her mother. Her mother and I had separated after about nine years of marriage. It's been close to three years now since it happened. In fact, my daughter would've been twelve on the fifth of next month.

"A man by the named Eric Whitepole, who had served more than ten years in prison for raping a ten-year-old, was released on good behavior. I guess they thought he was no longer a threat to society.

"After being free for about six months, he apparently decided to enact start raping children again. He spotted my daughter walking home from school and began a two-week vigil, learning as much as he could about her without drawing any attention to himself. He stalked my child patiently each day and planned her abduction, rape and murder— and no one suspected he was as evil as evil could be.

"He had an uncommonly attractive smile. I'll never forget the arrogance he projected at his trial while defending himself as his own attorney. He continuously denied that he had anything to do with it. He paced back and forth; smiling at the jurors and assuring them that this was a blatant case of mistaken identity.

"On the third of November, he pried my daughter's bedroom window open while she was sound asleep. Her mother was asleep in her room and was unaware that a snake had entered the house.

"After being found guilty, he finally confessed to what had happen that cold winter night. Combining his final confession to the prison psychiatrist and the trial manuscripts, I was able to piece together a story that has haunted me since that day.

"What I am about to tell you is how I've played it in my mind at least a thousand times. I've been trying desperately to ease some of my pain and anger by going through it again and again, but it only angers me more. This is how I think it went. I think he woke my daughter up and told her I'd asked him to come and pick her up. He told her I wanted to see her so we could plan a surprise party for her mother.

"They left the house through the back door and got into his car, which was parked in the alley. He was aware that the local police didn't patrol this part of town in the middle of the night. Once he got her into the back of his car, he immediately began to force himself upon her, savagely raping her and choking her until she was unconscious.

"Realizing he'd finally fulfilled his sexual fantasy, he began to complete his plan to dispose of her body. He drove nearly 10 miles out of town. I'm sure he looked on my daughter's battered body with pride as he drove and gloated over his sexual conquest. I can almost see her regaining consciousness and begging him to let her go.

"He pulled his car off the road and out of sight of the roadway. I can hear him saying, 'I've got to kill you now, Chelsea. If I don't they'll put me away forever. I really didn't mean to do it. I'm only 37 and don't want to spend 100 years in the slam.'

"He removed her body from the car and laid her against a chain link fence. Then, he got back into his car and drove away, stopping at every stop sign and obeying every law on his way back into Johnstown. He ate a hearty breakfast at a local Eat-n-Park, taking his time and holding a casual conversation with a young waitress.

"He paid his bill and drove to a car wash, where he cleaned out the inside and vacuumed the seats for more than an hour.

"In the mean time, the daylight exposed my daughter's small torn body to an early morning fisherman. The police were called immediately and they began a search for the car a trucker who had parked about fifty yards from the scene had noticed. The trucker had been curious enough to write down the tag number as Eric's car sped off just before daybreak.

"The yelling fisherman made him aware of what had happened. They wisely put two and two together and reported it to the police over the trucker's two-way radio. Within minutes, a police officer spotted Eric and his car at the car wash, and that's where they took him into custody without any resistance.

"The cops said he acted all innocent and tried to make it a white police against a black man thing. The whole time he kept saying he hadn't done anything.

"During the trial, he repeatedly said something like, 'It wasn't me. I was just washing my car when they arrested me because I'm black. How could they arrest me without proof? I would never harm a child. I don't even know the child. No one has come forward to say they saw me with that child. Their just saying it's me because of something I was arrested for a long time ago, and I didn't do that either. I served those years as an innocent man. Why would I do that to a child? Look at me. I can get any woman I want. I don't have to rape children. I swear to God that it was not me.'

"With the DNA, and other positive evidence, including tire prints, and the truckers sighting of his car, the jurors were 99% sure that he was a murdering rapist. The thing that sealed his fate though, in my opinion, what the hidden camera footage of him masturbating in his cell right after the attorney showed him pictures of my daughter's broken body!

"Their verdict was guilty and he was sentenced to 177 years in prison. That wasn't enough for what he did. I want him to die by my hands. I want vengeance to be mine. I want him to suffer slowly. I haven't been able to forgive myself for not being there to save her from the clutches of that evil sick bastard."

"My God, that's so awful!" Helen exclaimed. "I'm so, so sorry." She reached over and held Jason's hand. "I had no idea you'd seen that kind of evil." Helen stopped the car, and turned to the big man and opened her arms. "Come here," she said. "Let me hold you for a moment."

Like a boy, the big courageous man shyly leaned over and received her hug of compassion.

"It wasn't your fault," she said. "These evil men are like cancer. They strike without mercy and there seems to be nothing that can stop them or cure the disease. It truly wasn't your fault. That evil has been walking among us for thousands of years. It will not be easy to rid the world of pedophiles, but we will some day. I'm confident we will win."

PART FOUR

# UNSUNG HEROES

# CHAPTER 32

Helen and Jason arrived and parked across the street from the elementary school. "Now, all we've got to do is spot Sissy. She leaves by that green door on the left side of the school. I didn't know that at first and waited on the other side of the building and missed her. She finally told me which door to watch."

"What does she look like?" Jason asked.

"She's thin and kind of tall for a nine-year-old. She still wears braids with a part up the middle. She's about my complexion. She usually walks alone, with her head down. There she is. She's the one in the red jacket."

Helen got out of the car and called out, "Sissy! Sissy! Hey, little sister, over here."

Sissy recognized the familiar voice and it immediately brought a rare smile to her face. Sissy stepped up her pace and began to quickly walk toward her sister. They met on the sidewalk and embraced each other.

"Hey, little sister. I'm so glad to see you."

"Me too," Sissy said.

"Are you all right? I miss you like you wouldn't believe. You're on my mind constantly," Helen said as she hugged Sissy again. "I want you to meet a very good friend of mine," she said as she took Sissy's hand and began to walk toward Jason.

As they got a little closer, Sissy slowed her pace and looked around nervously up and down the street, watching for Floyd's truck.

"Come on, babe, believe me, he's not going to hurt you. He's a good friend and a good man."

Jason was leaning against the car as Sissy slowly approached with Helen kind of pulling her along.

"Jason, I want you to meet my sister, Sissy. Sissy, this is Jason. He's my friend, which means that he is also your friend."

"Hello," Jason said and reached his hand out to greet Sissy. "I've heard a lot about you. Your sister praises you as her most prized person in all the world. You must be very special."

"Hello," Sissy said, reaching out her hand to shake his and quickly bringing it back to her side.

"Jason wants to take you and me to Eat-n-Park. He's promised he'll have us back before your mom even misses you. What do you think? Should we take him up on it?"

"I don't know," Sissy answered hunching her shoulders.

"Please? I'll go in with you and explain to your mom if you want," Helen said.

"I don't know," Sissy shyly answered.

"I'll tell you what. You're right. Maybe it wouldn't be a good idea. Let's go sit in the playground and talk, and maybe Jason will go and get us something good to eat and we can all eat it there. Is that a better idea?"

"Okay," Sissy said, while pulling Helen away from Jason and toward the school playground.

"Get us something good, would you? We'll be right here when you get back," Helen said to Jason.

Jason got into the car and drove off as Sissy and Helen found seats on the playground bench.

"So what do you think of our friend Jason?"

"He's so big!"

"Yeah, that's exactly what I thought when we first met. He has the broadest shoulders I've ever seen. With that curly hair and mustache I kinda thought to myself, hmm he's a big guy, but he's pretty easy on the eyes.

Between you and me, he gets more and more charming as you get to know him," Helen said with a devilish grin on her face.

"Do you like him?"

"You know what, little sis? I've discovered that as our friendship grows, I care for him, more and more. He makes me feel special. And, God knows he is *so* nice to me. He has daughters that he loves and cares for in a way you and I had from our so-called dad. He would never harm them in anyway. In fact, he'd protect them with his life."

"Are they like me?" Sissy asked.

"What do you mean?"

"I mean, are they little girls or are they older?"

"They're older, but still a lot like you in many ways. They are warm hearted and kind and pretty like you, but they're kind of spoiled by their daddy. What have you been doing lately, little sister? I know you've been getting all those A's and B's, but has your mom been treating you nice and keeping Floyd away from you?"

"I guess"

"I wish I could take you home with me. It would make me so happy to know that you're all right and safe in my home. I brought you something," she said, pulling out a necklace and with a gold heart charm from her purse.

"Wow!" Sissy said. "Is it mine?"

"Of course it's yours. I hope you'll cherish it forever because it means I love you. Turn around and let me put it on you."

Sissy stood holding the small heart against her chest as Helen struggled with the clasp. Sissy wasn't saying a word, but she had a huge smile on her face. When Helen finally secured the necklace, Sissy turned around and raised both arms for a hug.

"Thank you, big sister. I've never had a necklace before. I just love it so much. I'm gonna wear it 'til I die."

"You're welcome, babe. It's a token of my affection for you. I want you to know that this necklace and charm is something you can hold in your hand that shows the love I have for you as my sister. I want you to know that love is something you can grasp with your heart, just as I have. I want you to always recognize the difference. And I want you to always know that love is God-sent and will never go away or be lost. No matter what happens, we'll always be connected to each other, and nobody can undo our bond. Okay?

"On a lighter note, we've got to find a way to stay in touch with each other so I can know you're all right and you can know I'm all right. I'm going to give you my phone number again and Jason's, too. I want you to memorize them. Can you do that for me, little sis?"

"Yes," Sissy answered.

"If I'm ever in trouble, I'm going to call my little sister to come to my rescue, but I want you to do the same. Okay?"

"Okay."

"I hope Jason gets back soon. I'm hungry. How 'bout you?"

"A little bit."

"Well, look who's coming with the good stuff," Helen loudly said while pointing at Jason who was walking toward them carrying three bags of food. He had a big wide grin on his face.

"It's about time. Where'd you go, Timbuktu?"

"No, it took a while to find a place good enough for my two princess friends."

"Oh, wow!" Helen said. "You got all this for me and little sis or do you plan on feedin' your face, too?" she joked with a smile.

"I hope you guys can throw me a couple of crumbs. How bout it, little sister?" Jason asked while looking at Sissy.

"I guess so."

"Oh, come on! You can do better than that!"

"Okay, you can eat some," Sissy shyly said.

"Now we're talkin'!"

The three of them ate and talked about school and music and other safe topics for nearly an hour. Sissy had become comfortable with Jason, especially since her big sister trusted him so much. She even showed them the latest dance steps she'd seen on TV.

Sissy looked up at Helen, whose expression had changed. She stood up on the bench to see what Helen was looking at, while Jason was humming a popular song.

Suddenly Sissy's expression changed and she jumped down from the bench. She'd looked down the block and seen a pick-up truck that looked like Floyd's. "I gotta go!" she said nervously. "I gotta get home now."

Helen looked at her, and without a word Sissy scurried through the schoolyard toward home.

"Bye, little sister."

"Bye," Sissy said without looking back.

"Remember what I said and remember the numbers. Okay?"

"Okay," Sissy said, again without stopping or looking back.

The two of them watched as she hurried away, both knowing she was afraid, and both feeling a sense of helplessness.

"Hey," Jason said. "It'll be all right. She'll be all right because you'll always be around for her. Come on, buddy, let's head back. I enjoyed this time with you and your little sister. She reminds me so much of Chelsea. I can see why you're so attached to her. Don't make the mistake I made and take your eyes off her long enough for that asshole to do anymore damage."

"I won't. I just don't know what I can do. Praying is not enough. I wish I could take her away from them. I just don't know how."

## CHAPTER 33

"I seen you. You oughta know by now, I'm everywhere. I thought we told you to stay away from that bitch!"

"She's my sister and I don't have to," Sissy said in an unusually bold voice.

"Who you think you talkin' to, you little heifer?"

Sissy suddenly realized she might have said too much. She lowered her head without answering and tried to go out the front door.

"Oh, no you don't!" Floyd said. "Get your butt upstairs and go ta bed. I'm gonna go get yo momma and tell her where you been. Hangin' out there wit that woman and some man. We don't know what that man might a done to you. You in big trouble!"

"He was nice and he's my sister's friend. He's not like you." Again, Sissy realized that she might've said too much. As Floyd's eyes blazed with rage, she ran up the steps crying.

Floyd got into his truck and drove by the school to see if Helen and her friend were still there. They weren't. He continued to a home a few blocks down North Avenue where Hazel was visiting one of her friends. Floyd blew his horn and motioned to Hazel to come on. Instead, Hazel came out onto the porch and told Floyd that she and her friend were going out to South Park for a few hours and she'd see him later.

"You betta get yo ass in this truck. We got somethin' ta talk about."

"No, I said I'll see you later!" Hazel yelled as she gestured for him to leave and went back into her friend's house. Floyd sped off in anger and headed back home.

"Okay," said to himself. "I'll take care of it my damn self. Don't nobody mistreat or disrespect me like dat. I'll teach 'em both a little lesson."

Sissy peeked out of her mother's bedroom window when she heard Floyd's truck pull up. She panicked when she saw Floyd's angry look as he slammed his truck door shut hard enough to rock the truck back and forth. She ran back into her room, shut the door, and put a box in front of it to keep him from coming in. She climbed into her bed fully dressed and hid her head under the covers.

She was scared and trembling. "Oh no," she whispered. "Oh no, please don't let him come in here." Like so many times before, she heard the back door slam. She somehow knew that the man downstairs was no longer just Floyd. Now he was Floyd possessed by evil. Her soul cried out for Ozz and Chism to help her through another night. She knew they were there.

Like before, each step Floyd took seemed to take an eternity. As he reached the landing, she squeezed her eyes shut. "Please don't come in here. Please just go away."

Floyd turned the doorknob and pushed against the box she had put against the door. He laughed. "That's what I like. You knew I was coming. That means you got it ready for me." He shoved a little harder and the box slid aside. "Ole Floyd's here, baby, and I got to punish you a little tonight for what you did. You made Ole Floyd mad. You and yo momma made me real mad. So now you gotta make it up to me."

Sissy was lying as still as she could. *I'm not in here. I'm sleep. Maybe he won't see me!* she thought desperately and squeezed her eyes shut so tight that she began to see a rainbow of colors behind her eyelids. She tried to pass out and avoid his vicious onslaught. "No!" she cried out. "Leave me alone."

In one strong quick move, Floyd yanked the blanket off the her, leaving her curled up with her fist still clenched closed and her eyes shut so tight that she was shaking from muscle tension. "No!" she cried out. "Leave me alone."

Floyd stood at the foot of the bed, gazing down at his prey. He was filled with a lust that is unknown to a normal man. Sissy's fear was his foreplay. He watched as the small child trembled. "Oh, yeah!" he said aloud. "Oh yeah, its gonna hurt! Its gonna hurt a lot dis time. Your daddy would turn over in his grave to feel the joy we gonna share. I hope you ready for yo best thrill ever!"

Sissy continued to tremble. Ozz and Chism were there but could not bear to stay. They felt a presence of evil that was slowly reaching its highest level of existence."

"We must leave here or we will burst inside and cease to be. My anger has taken me beyond its limits. I'm dying of hate," said Ozz.

"I to am boiling inside to the point of cursing our God. You are right. We must leave this place and go back to heaven, for to watch this is certainly to be in hell," remarked Chism.

Sissy felt her two archangels departing from her. "No!" she said. "Don't leave me!" she cried to no avail. They'd left the room so quickly it caused the windowpane and furniture to rattle.

"Mine!" said Floyd. "You're mine. My sweet, sweet little virgin, you make me feel so strong. Someday, little lady, you'll wish that I would do this for you again and again." He reached out and slapped her as hard as he could across her clothed bottom.

Sissy didn't move. She continued to tremble more and more uncontrollably. Floyd undid the zipper on his coveralls and continued to stand above her with himself in his hand. "Come on, little girl, help Floyd out." He grabbed her fragile ankle and yanked her legs open.

"*No!*" she screamed. "No, I hate you!" She kicked and squirmed violently. Floyd grabbed her entire face in his right hand and squeezed her face as hard as he could.

"That's my girl! Beg for Floyd. I hate it when you lay there and pretend to be asleep." Floyd's voice roared and sounded unearthly.

Sissy struggled hard to get free. She felt like she was fighting for her life. After a few minutes, she lay still, panting from exhaustion. Floyd had yet to make his intended thrust.

"No!" he said as he slapped her cheeks from side to side. "No! Don't you go to sleep this time. No!" Balled his hand into a loose fist and struck her harder than he could ever remember hitting anyone.

"Did you like that man you seen today? Did you want him, too? Do you like what yo daddy did to ya? Do you like me? Did you want him too?"

Sissy began to vomit, as she became more and more faint. He grabbed her face again and twisted it as he continued to talk. "You little bitch! You wanted to be unfaithful to Floyd. Now we'll make you know who owns you. Now you're gonna be punished for giving it to your daddy! Now you're gonna beg for Floyd. Beg, you little bitch, beg!" he shouted as he pounded on her.

"Say you love me and I'll take it easy. Go head, say it! No you don't. You're not gonna go to sleep on me this time!" he shouted as he had his way with her.

Sissy had passed out long before Floyd punished her little helpless body with the filth of his orgasm. Floyd fell asleep soon after, grunting and snorting like a hog.

Sissy regained consciousness and made her way to the bathroom, carrying her clothes. She slumped against the closed door for a moment and breathed as deeply as she could. She dressed her battered body and ran down the stairs and out the front door. *I'm running away,* she thought. *I'm running to find my sister and I'm never coming back!"*

# CHAPTER 34

Night had fallen when Hazel returned home to find Floyd asleep in Sissy's bloody bed.

"Oh my God, Floyd! What've you done?"

"Huh?" Floyd mumbled as he woke and began to gather his thoughts. "It wouldn't me! I seen Sissy wit some man at the school playground. And when I came home after seein' you, I found da room like dis. I been layin' here cryin', hopin' she all right. I don't know what happen here! I swear! Ask her. She'll tell you herself. There was a man up here! Just ask her!"

"She's not here! I looked all over the house and she's not here!" Hazel said. "We got to call the police!"

"No, Hazel! Don't call da police. I'll find her. She cain't be far. I'll find her and that son of a bitch and kill him!"

Floyd left the house and went up to the school playground, looking for Sissy. He was hoping to find her first and threaten to kill her mother if she said anything about what he had done to her, just as he always did. He questioned a lady that lived across the street from the playground with a suggestive lie. "Did you see my little stepdaughter on the playground earlier wit a big light skinned man? He took her from my house and beat and maybe raped her. Did you see him?"

"Yeah, but I thought there was a woman with her," the lady responded.

"No, dare wouldn't no woman. Dat was him. The woman left dem alone. Do you remember what dat man look like?"

"Yeah, there was a big light skinned guy in a red sporty car. It must've been him. That dirty stinkin' dog! Yeah, I remember what he look like. That bastard! Elma, next door seen him too, 'cause she was saying he sure looked good! That dirty dog. I hope they cut his balls off! Yeah, I know exactly what he looked like!" she repeated.

Floyd looked up and down the dark streets to no avail. He finally went back to the house and confronted Hazel. "Baby, that lady up by the school said she seen Sissy wit a tall light skinned guy and a couple of her neighbors seen him too. Dey said it looked like he drove her this way right after school. He must've beat and raped her in our own house."

"Oh, God!" Hazel said. "We gotta find my baby! Go find her! My baby! That no-good bastard!"

"Don't call da police, baby, 'cause I don't want 'em to blame it on me. Kids try ta blame things on their momma's boyfriend when they know they done wrong. We gotta make her tell da police who dat guy was and not protect him. One of dem ladies up by da school said dat man's been meetin' her up at da playground and givin' her things for a couple of weeks. She must've brought him home. I'm gonna kill him if he harmed our little Sissy!" Floyd said while nervously rubbing his hands together.

# CHAPTER 35

When the police arrived, they were given a description of the man seen with Sissy at the playground. They thoroughly examined Sissy's bedroom and completed a full report of what they found, including the gold chain and heart that Hazel said she'd never seen before.

The police questioned several neighbors, asking if they'd seen the big man fitting the description Floyd had gave. They confirmed they had seen the man standing by his red car and later at the playground. Sissy was yet to be found by Floyd or the police.

# CHAPTER 36

Little Sissy made her way up North Avenue, then turned down N. Wood Street past the local donut shop and on down to Kelly Street. She found a pay phone there. She picked up the receiver and dialed the number Helen had given her.

"Hello? Hello?" she said into the phone. There was no answer. "Hello, big sister?" still no answer. She dialed again with the same results. Sissy sat down under the pay phone wondering what to do. An old lady came up and put a quarter in and dialed her number. She talked on the phone and occasionally glanced down at Sissy.

"Please, can you make a call for me?" Sissy asked the lady.

"Shame on your mother, little girl. You have no business being out this late begging. I'm going to give you a quarter but you tell your mother or who ever it is watching you that next time I'll call the police. Here," she said, and handed Sissy the coin.

"Thank you."

Again, Sissy tried the number. This time with the payment, the phone began to ring. It range six times, and there was no answer. She waited a while and tried again, still no answer. She tried again and again. Finally, she sat back down on the curb. The chill of the night was beginning to be uncomfortable. She tried to remember Jason's number, but she wasn't sure if the last number was a two or a four, and she only had one quarter.

She called Helen's number once more, but there was still no answer. She decided to take a chance and dial what she thought was Jason's number. The number rang four times and was answered by a voice machine. *"You have reached Jason. Please leave a message at the beep. I will return your call as soon as possible."*

Sissy didn't know what to say or do. "Hello, big sister," she said. "This is Sissy. Floyd has hurt me and I'm running away. Can you help me? I'm at a big stone building at the pay phone. I'm a pretty long way from home and its cold. Hello? Please come and get me, big sister ... good bye."

Jason and Helen had attended a business meeting at the Washington Hilton that lasted until 11 p.m. Jason dropped Helen off at her home shortly afterward. They talked for about an hour and Jason bid her good night and headed for his home in Alexandria. It was nearly 1 a.m. when he finally got home for the night. He noticed the phone message light was blinking and had recorded fifteen calls.

"Not tonight," he said to himself. "I'll answer my messages tomorrow when I'm rested." With that thought, he got ready to go to bed. The phone rang just as he was about to lay down.

"Hello?"

"Hey, its me. Did you get my message?" Helen asked.

"What message?"

"I left you a message just saying thank you for going with me to see my sister. I forgot to thank you once we started talking about business, so I left a little message. I guess you got home yet."

"Oh, you're welcome. No, I didn't get the message. I'd decided to wait until morning to deal with my messages."

"Okay. Well, thanks again. I guess I'll see you on the job site tomorrow."

"Okay, Helen. You sleep well and don't worry; it'll be all right I promise you. Take care, my girl," he said shyly flirting. "Good night."

Jason curled up, ready to sleep, but then decided it would be nice to hear Helen's voice again. He also wondered what she'd said in her message. He dialed into his recorder and listened to the last message.

"Hello, big sister," said the child's voice, causing Jason to sit up right in surprise. He listened to Sissy's message while his heart pounded, then immediately called Helen.

"Helen, something's wrong with Sissy. She left a message on my machine about an hour ago."

"My God, Jason! What did she say? Where is she?"

"She said Floyd had hurt her and she ran away. She said she was at a pay phone in front of a big stone building. I'm going over to that area as soon as I get off the phone. There can't be that many stone buildings with a pay phone at the front. I'm going to check place I can find. I'll find her. Don't worry. In the meantime, call the police."

"I will. I'll call the police and her mother so I can find out what happened. Call me the minute you find her. I'll stay right here by the phone. Please, Jason, find her for me."

Jason's route took him right up North Wood St. Unknowingly he glanced at the pay phone Sissy had made her calls from, but he didn't see her. Ironically she'd moved into the bank's entry cove where it was warmer and she couldn't be seen from the street.

Jason continued looking at the location of every pay phone he could recall seeing in the area. He checked one after another without seeing any sign of her. Two hours had passed before he stopped to call Helen.

"Hey, I've looked everywhere, at every pay phone and every stone building that looked like it should have a pay phone. I can't find her."

"The police are looking for her, too. Her mother was frantic; saying someone had raped and kidnapped her. Listen, Jason, she said the police are looking for a big man in a red sports car that Sissy was seen with at the elementary school early today."

"What? You've got to be kidding me! What's going on, Helen?"

"I don't know. I'm going to the police station to find out. I'll call you as soon as I know something."

"No, I think I'd better go to the police station myself. I'll meet you there in about twenty minutes. I guess the nearest station is East Liberty. I'm at Penn Avenue and North Braddock. I'm going to look for her on the way."

"Okay. I'll see you there. That poor child must be going through hell. I just pray that she's all right."

Jason turned onto North Wood Street, looking from side to side. Once again he slowly passed the bank where Sissy was sitting. He paused as he spotted what looked like a small bundle of blankets, and then continued on. Something urged him to pull over and walk back to the pay phone in front of the bank he had just passed.

He looked around the side of the building as he passed the pay phone. Nothing. He started back to his car when he glanced at the small pile of clothes — it moved. Jason's heart filled with hope as he walked up to the bundle and realized it was Sissy. He quickly knelt down on one knee and lifted her into his arms.

"Hey there, precious," he said. "I am so glad to see you. Are you all right, little one?"

"Yes," Sissy answered and shivered. "I'm just cold. Where's my sister?"

"It's all right now, babe, I've got you. She's waiting for you. She'll be so glad to know that I've found you."

He put her into the car and went to the pay phone to call and see if Helen had left for the police station yet.

"Hello?" Helen said.

"Helen, its me again. Guess what? I found her!" Jason said while nearly being overwhelmed with tears of joy. "I found her curled up in the entryway of the bank on North Wood Street. She's all right, but Floyd has beaten her up pretty bad. Her little face is bruised and swollen and she's cold, but I think she's going to be all right."

"That bastard! Bring her here, Jason. Please, bring her here."

"I'll be there in ten minutes, but I think we should take her to Children's Hospital."

"Okay, you're right. Pick me up. I'll be outside when you get here," Helen said and hung up the phone. "Thank you God! Thank you for letting him find her! Thank you! Thank you so, so much!"

Helen rushed to the door to wait for Jason's car to pull up. In a few moments that seemed like hours, he drove into the driveway. Helen got into the backseat where Sissy was sleeping. She pulled her sister into her arms and hugged her tightly.

"Oh, baby. I'm so, so glad to be able to hold you. I was so worried I thought I'd die."

"Hi, big sister," Sissy said sleepily.

Helen reared back a little to look into Sissy's bruised face. "Oh baby, who did this to you?"

"Floyd got mad at me because he seen me with you, so he punished me. He hurt me, big sister — worse than ever before. I hate him so much!"

"I know, baby. I hate him, too. He's not going to get away with this, not this time. I'll see to that. We're going to take you to the hospital and make sure you're okay. Let me just hold you. I'm so sorry, baby. I wouldn't ever do anything to cause you harm." Helen broke down and to cried.

Jason quietly listened to the two of them with tears rolling down his manly face as he drove as fast as he could to Children's Hospital.

"Big sister, my teeth are cutting into my lip. I think they are coming out," Sissy said.

"It'll be all right babe. We'll be there in a few minutes. Be strong for me, okay?" She squeezed Sissy tighter against her chest.

"Poor, baby," Jason angrily blurted out. "I can't believe that fool would do this and think he's going to get away with it. Not this time! This time he's gonna pay, even if I've gotta get that payment myself. In fact, I'd rather look him in the eyes and make him pay with my own two hands, he said as they pulled up to the hospital. "Let's get her inside," he said and jumped out of the car to hurriedly opened the back door and pick up Sissy.

"Come on, kid. Its gonna be all right now. They'll take good care of you, and your big sister will be right here by your side."

"Jason's right, honey. I'll be right here with you. Just try not to worry. Okay?"

As Jason sat the waiting room, two plainclothes police officers approached and identified themselves. "Sir, are you the one that brought Miss Williams to the hospital?"

"Yes," answered Jason.

"Sir, you are under arrest. Do you have a weapon on you?"

"No. Why are you arresting me? Why aren't you arresting Floyd?"

"Sir, please turn around and put your hands high against the wall," one of the officers said, as the other began to search Jason. "You are under arrest for child abuse. I need to read you your rights. Do you understand that anything you say can be used against you in the court of law?"

"Yes," Jason said as his hands were cuffed behind his back.

"What's going on here?" Helen asked when she came into the waiting room while Jason was being handcuffed. "Why are you arresting him?"

"Sorry, ma'am. Please stand back. We've got to take him in."

"Why? He hasn't done anything, you idiot. He's the one who found her. We brought her here."

"Please, ma'am, just stay back. You can come to the station and make your statement."

"No," Jason interrupted. "You stay right here with her and don't leave her side. I'll be all right. I'll call you as soon as I get this straightened out."

"Okay. I'm sorry Jason. I'll be there as soon as I know she's all right. He hasn't done anything, officers. You should be picking up that child rapist, Floyd," Helen remarked as the officer escorted Jason out the double doors.

# CHAPTER 37

After the doctor and several nurses tended to Sissy injuries, a police officer and a Child and Youth Services employee questioned her and determined from her statement that Floyd, not Jason, had violated the her. The CYS employee told Helen and Hazel, who had just arrived at Children's Hospital, that Floyd was the apparent assailant.

Hazel initially tried to deny the possibility, but after talking to Sissy she, too, realized that Floyd had done the unthinkable. He had now been exposed as the long-time child molester she knew he was.

"I'm sorry, Mrs. Williams. We'll have to keep your children with us until we're confident you can provide a safe environment for them," the lady from CYS said. "You will be expected to file charges against this Floyd fellow. In addition to the charges you file, we will file on behalf of the child and the State of Virginia. Are there any relatives who qualify to take temporary custody of the children?"

"No, our family has a few elderly aunts and uncles here in the Washington area, but they can't take care of no kids," Hazel answered.

"Excuse me," Helen interjected. "I'm Sissy's sister and I would be more than qualified and willing to take custody of Sissy. Just tell me what you need from me and I'll have it for you today."

"Is that acceptable to you, Mrs. Williams?" the CYS worker asked.

Hazel held her face in her hands without responding, while Helen waited anxiously to hear Hazel say yes.

"Mrs. Williams, is that acceptable to you or would you rather we take Sissy with us when she's released?"

Still, Hazel was silent.

"She's my sister and you know I would protect her with my life," Helen said, looking directly at Hazel who still had her face covered.

"I guess," Hazel finally responded. "But, how long will it be before I can get my children back?"

"I don't know, Mrs. Williams. That will be determined by the juvenile authorities once their investigation is complete."

"How can I press charges against Floyd? He'll kill me. I don't think he meant ta hurt Sissy. He been under a lot of pressure. He really not a bad man. He love Sissy," Hazel said.

"If that's what you think, Mrs. Williams, it will probably be a very long time before Sissy is allowed to come home. We'll also need to examine the other children to see if they've been harmed."

Turning to Helen, she said, I'll need your full name, address and phone number to complete the proper forms for temporary custody."

"Okay. Here is my driver's license and I'll provide whatever else you need. When can I take her home?"

"They're going to keep her here for a couple of days for observation. The paperwork should be complete by then. If everything is acceptable, we'll release her into your custody."

"Thank you," Helen said.

"Mrs. Williams, do you know where Floyd is right now?"

"He was home when I left. I think he still there. But I'm sure he didn't mean it. I need to talk to Sissy myself. Maybe she don't realize it was an accident or maybe it was somethin' she just imagined."

"Mrs. Williams, your child has been sexually assaulted. She's not imagining that or the cuts and bruises all over her body," said the policewoman.

"Well, maybe he jus need help. Like I said, he been under pressure," Hazel said.

With that, the police officer shook her head and went to make the call and to have Jason released and Floyd picked up for questioning. Helen went back toward the emergency area to see Sissy. She turned and saw Hazel step into a pay phone, so she turned around and stood close enough to listen to what Hazel said.

"Floyd, I don't know who did this to Sissy, but they think it was you. They on their way to arrest you. You better get outta there now. Go over to Judy's. I'll call you after I talk to Sissy and straighten this mess out. I'll talk to you later. I hope you learned from this Floyd. You oughta know by now that sometime you just go too far. All right. Good-bye."

As Hazel hung up the phone, Helen stepped back and out of sight. She watched as Hazel gathered herself and headed toward the room where Sissy was being attended. Helen was trying to keep her peace with Hazel so she could get custody of Sissy, but after hearing that conversation she was finding it hard to control her anger. *I can't believe she actually warned Floyd so he could avoid the cops. I've got to make Hazel accept that Floyd is a vicious and dangerous man who should never have access to Sissy again.*

"Hazel," Helen called out. "Can I speak to you for a moment?"

"I don't know, Helen. I'm not gonna listen to you talk bad about Floyd. He done a lot of good things for me since Henry died. It's hard for me to believe he hurt Sissy like that. She must have done somethin' to cause him to go off."

"I understand," Helen said. "I just want to take Sissy off your hands until Floyd calms down. You know, Ms. Hazel, I'm not saying to you that Floyd is a bad and evil man. I'm saying that Sissy is a good and innocent child, and for anyone to knowingly subject her to potential harm is an unforgivable sin. I know you must love her as you do your other children. But, for some reason as you and I both know, your late husband decided to make all three of us his living sex toys.

"It seems like you've turned your head in denial. You know and I know that Floyd has been doing evil to Sissy for a long time. In all fairness to Sissy, I think you and I should put a stop to it and give her a chance at childhood happiness and self-esteem. Come on, Hazel, what do you say? Let's take her out of his grasp."

"Floyd a good man. He only do that sort of thing when he feelin' down."

"Oh, please!" Helen said sarcastically, as she began to lose her cool. "That's bullshit. He does it because he likes to torment children. He does it because it makes him a big self-serving man. Let's face it. You're in love with a child rapist just like you were with my father. You can make excuses for them and all the other scum who do the same thing, but the truth is they should be castrated!"

Helen quickly tried to calm down. "Look, the important thing here is that Sissy is given a chance. Who knows what Floyd will do the next time he's *feeling down* and abusing Sissy's the only way he can feel better," she said sarcastically.

Hazel understood exactly what Helen was saying but she was in love with Floyd and hopelessly dependent on his dominance for her own sexual satisfaction. After so many years of fighting with Henry, she'd finally found the relationship she felt was meant for her. Hazel, now being older and indoctrinated with submissiveness, knew of no other options.

"Well, Sissy has never told me that Henry or Floyd ever touch her in that way. I'm not sure I believe you. But, you're right; somebody did this to my child. If Floyd had a couple of drinks and did it, he'll never drink in my house again. I know that."

"Here we go with the bullshit again. You know what, Hazel? I think we should just stay focused on Sissy. I don't care what you do with Floyd. There is no excuse big enough for him and what he did, and obviously there is no excuse too small for you to cling to."

"I'm just sayin' she never told me," Hazel responded defensively.

"What about Floyd's hints about being the one who strangled my mother? He even said that my father conspired with him and Bishop Jones to hide allegations that my father sexually abused me regularly. I know without a doubt. My father, your late husband, abused me. You know as well as I do that he did the same thing to Sissy."

"No, I don't know that. Sissy never told me," Hazel said, still sticking to her story.

"Did you know my mother or know of her? She was twenty-six when was murdered. Did you know my father married you less than a year later?

You were what, 12 when he swept you off your feet and you married him at 13. He was a 47-year-old man who'd been sexually molesting his own six-year-old daughter! Do you get the picture, Hazel? Do you see the possibility that my father moved from child to child?

"Maybe he taught Floyd the sick pleasures of child molesting. Who knows? I wonder how long he knew Floyd. Did he know Floyd when he was younger? Are you that blind, Hazel? More than likely, Floyd has spent more time sexually with Sissy than he's spent with you."

"No. You crazy! I don't believe a word you've said."

"Well, I hope you're right. Maybe Sissy hasn't been abused. Maybe my nightmares are just dreams. Or maybe these two men are a perfect example of loving and caring mates for *you*. If you believe that, then we have no reason to be concerned. But, if you have the slightest doubt, please let Sissy stay with me until you're sure she's safe."

"I said okay! I said she could stay wit you for a while. Leave it be!"

"Thank you, Hazel! You won't be sorry. I think Sissy is waiting for us. Let's go see her."

Helen and Hazel walked into the examination area to find Sissy sitting up and drinking ginger ale.

"Hello, baby," Hazel greeted her.

"Hi little, sister," came from Helen.

# CHAPTER 38

Three days after Sissy was admitted to Children's Hospital, she was released. Hazel, contrary to what CYS had said, was the one who was called to take her home. The nine-year-old was delighted to get back to her family. She even seemed to forget everything that had happened. She was greeted as if she'd been away for years instead of a few days. For that brief moment, she felt special.

At school there were twisted stories of what had happened but her peers continued on as if nothing ever happened. Floyd was released on bail less in than twenty-four hours, thanks to Hazel putting up the house as part of the bond. As part of his release agreement, Floyd had to participate in group therapy with others who'd been accused of molesting or abusing a family member.

\*\*\*

A short time passed and Floyd began to fit back into the family. Even Sissy had begun to think that Floyd had 'learned his lesson,' and was no longer a threat. Children are innocent and they forgive quickly. Often, they forget the bad things that happen to them entirely. They anxiously resume their lives and make the best of their environment.

In the meantime, Helen was furious with CYS. She argued with them that it was ludicrous to send Sissy back to a home where Floyd would eventually take advantage of her again. ' Her voice fell on closed ears. After a few weeks she began to back down on her threats and hope for the best for Sissy.

She called twice a week and asked if she could speak with Sissy, but Hazel would not permit Sissy to come to the phone.

*\*\*\**

Three months had passed and Helen had all but given up on the chance of speaking to Sissy. She drove to the elementary school a couple times a week to try to talk to her. The few days Helen did see Sissy, she was being escorted home by Hazel or an adult female Helen had never met.

Nearly four months after Sissy's hospitalization, Hazel called Helen's home on a cold winter night.

"Helen?" Hazel asked. "Where's Sissy? If you have her, I'm gonna have you arrested!"

"What are you talking about? I've been trying for months just to talk to her on the phone!"

"Well, she wasn't home when I got in today."

"She's not with me and I haven't heard from her. Where's Floyd?" Helen asked.

"I knew you'd try ta put the blame on Floyd. For your information, he right here wit me and just as worried as me. Him and Sissy been getting along fine. I'm warning you, if we don't have her here with us in the next hour, we're gonna call the cops!"

"I haven't even talked to her since that day at the hospital. Have you searched for her at the school playground?"

"Yeah, we've checked the playground and with some of the other kids that walk this way."

"I suggest you don't wait, call the police right now. I'm coming over there. I'm going to help you find her." Helen hung up before Hazel could respond and called Jason.

"Jason? It's me. Sissy's missing again. She never made it home from school."

"Oh, no! What can I do?"

"Would you please take me over there? Maybe we can ride around the area or something. I want to look for her. Do you mind doing that for me?"

"I'll do it for you and me. I'm on my way. I'll pick you up in about twenty minutes."

"Hey, Jason, thank you. You always seem to be there when I ask. I hope I'll be able to do the same for you if you're ever in need."

"If I'm ever in need you're the first person I'd count on. Don't worry, we found her before and we'll find her again. If that piece of shit Floyd has hurt her again, I'll personally break his black neck!"

By the time Jason and Helen got to Sissy's neighborhood it was nearly 10 p.m., and the temperature had dropped below freezing.

"Where do we start? There's no one out on the streets to ask. We can't just walk around looking in dark corners."

"I don't know," answered Helen.

"Well, you're a girl. Where would you go on a cold winter night?"

"One thing's for sure, I wouldn't go far from home — especially when it's so cold. If she had gone to a friend's house I'm sure someone would've called. You know, on second thought, I'm becoming more and more concerned. I was thinking that if she was in trouble she would've called me like she did before."

"Let's think it through. If you'd left school and were on your way home, where might you stop?"

"Nowhere," Helen said. "As you see, there's nowhere to stop. Let's park down there by her house." As they slowly drove towards Sissy's home, Helen said," I don't see a police car. I wonder if they've called the police yet. They're probably just sitting in there on their lazy asses. I'm going in there," she said as she opened the car door.

"I'm going with you. Maybe she's home and all will end well. Let's go," Jason said and slammed his car door closed.

Helen knocked on the front door and waited for someone to answer. She looked up at Jason and impatiently turned around and knocked again; this time much harder. She could hear the television playing inside when she stood closer and listened for some sign of life. Helen turned the doorknob and the door sprung open.

"Hello?" she shouted into the house.

There was no answer, so she stepped inside and shouted again. "Hello? Is anybody here?" She heard some frantic rumbling and whispering just before Hazel appeared at the top of the steps buttoning up her blouse.

"I'm here. We were just up here trying to figure out where Sissy might be," she said while doing her final touches on her collar and fastening her belt.

*Yeah, right,* Helen thought but said, "I didn't mean to just barge in. I do apologize, but the door was open and no one answered. We were looking for Sissy in the area and decided to stop in see if you or the police had heard anything."

"No, we haven't found her yet, or I should say, she hasn't come home yet. We ain't called the police 'cause we think she might be over a friend's house or somethin'. Her and Floyd had some sort of little disagreement and she left the house mad and said she wasn't never comin' back. I didn't want those CYS people thinkin' she was running away 'cause that would jus get her in trouble. You know what I mean?"

"No, I don't know what you mean," Helen said. "What kind of little disagreement did Floyd have with the nine-year-old child?"

"None of your business, bitch!" Floyd yelled from the top of the steps. "You ain't got nothin' ta do wit it. She probably got kidnapped or somethin' tryin' to get over to you."

"It is my business; she's my sister. And, I'm not a bitch. You're the bitch — someone who rapes and beats children," Helen bravely said as Floyd began to storm down the steps toward her.

Floyd hadn't seen Jason, who was still standing just outside the door. But, by the time he reached the bottom of the stairs, Jason was standing inside and directly in front of Helen.

"Well, big bad Floyd, don't stop now," Jason taunted.

When Floyd realized Jason was with Helen, he quickly turned and went halfway back up the steps.

"Who's the bitch now?" Jason asked.

"I think you people should get outta our house 'fore I put a bullet in ya both," Floyd said.

"Are you threatening me, Floyd? I thought you just did that to women and children. If you bring a gun out, I'm going to shove it right up your child molesting ass!"

"Oh? You think so, huh? I got news for you," Floyd said addressing Jason. "I fucked her and I fucked her better than her daddy did and I helped her daddy please her just like we did dat little bitch behind you. Ask her did she like it as much as Sissy likes it? Go head! Ask her!" Floyd shouted at the top of his lungs. "Ask her!"

As Floyd turned and started to go back up stairs, but Jason lunged forward and grabbed his coveralls. "You piece of shit!" Jason said through gritted teeth as he tried to pull Floyd back down the stairs. Floyd, twisted and yanked himself out of Jason's grasp and ran up the stairs, pushing Hazel down the stairs onto Jason.

"Jason, no!" Helen shouted as Hazel came tumbling onto his chest.

"Get out of my house!" Hazel screamed. "Get out, I said! Get out right now!"

"Come on, Jason! He might have a gun or something! Just come on, I don't want you to get hurt! He's not worth it!"

Floyd had gone into the front bedroom but came back to the top of the steps, taunting Jason, "Come on up here, I got somethin' for you, big hero!"

Just as Helen pulled Jason out of the front door the house exploded with three booming shots from the weapon Floyd held in his hand.

Hazel screamed, "Oh my God, Floyd! What're you doin'?"

"Shut up, you stupid bitch!" he said, as he fired twice more directly down the stairs. Hazel fell hard against the door and slid down out onto the floor of the porch at Helen and Jason's feet.

"That fool shot her!" Jason said while bending over Hazel and attempting to drag her aside while keeping a cautious eye on Floyd. "Come on, Hazel. We're going to get you to a hospital. Can you stand?"

Hazel tried to talk but only blurted out incoherent words and began to shake.

"She's going into shock!" Helen said. "We've got to get help, Jason. She's hurt bad!"

Helen reached behind Hazel to give a hand in lifting her up. Her hand slipped into a gaping hole the size of her fist just below the back of her Hazel's neck. "Oh God!" Helen screamed. "It's much worse than I thought!"

"Help me lift her. We've got to get her to the hospital. Now!" Jason said as he turned to find Floyd standing in the doorway, not three feet away.

"You ain't takin' her nowhere!" Floyd shouted as he pointed the gun in Jason's face.

"No! Please, no!" Helen screamed.

Jason stood up and tackled Floyd before he could get off a shot. They struggled for a few seconds, then Floyd squealed and slipped away. He ran out onto the street, while Hazel held onto Jason's coat as tightly as she could to keep him from following. Even as she lay there shot by Floyd, she was still protecting him.

"Let him go, Jason. The police will get him now. He's not worth it," Helen pleaded.

"Go in and call an ambulance for Hazel," Jason told Helen. "Let's get help for her and hopefully I'll have another at Floyd or maybe he'll get what he deserves from the police."

Helen ran into the house and called 911 to report what had happened. After her call she returned to the front porch. It had begun to snow hard, and Jason had taken off his coat to cover what was now Hazel's nearly dead and jerking body. He sat shivering, clutching her in his blood soaked lap. Jason's head hung to his chest as he realized a person had died as the result of a few moments of stupidity.

The ambulance arrived, followed a short time later by the Coroner, a slew of police officers, and the media. Helen and Jason stood dumbfounded as they tried to answer question after question from the police.

Through it all, Helen worried where Sissy was. Jason too kept looking out into the snowy night wondering the same thing. He hoped she wasn't cold and alone.

# CHAPTER 39

After hours of questioning at the local precinct, Helen and Jason left the police station together. It was just about daybreak and people were beginning to get out and about for another typical day in the Wood Street section of Washington.

On the way home, they decided to drive by Sissy's house one more time. Floyd's truck was parked where it had been when the night before. It was covered with snow and untouched. They noticed an unmarked police car about half a block away, presumably watching Floyd's truck.

"Where do you think he is?"

"I don't know. I hope he's fallen in a river or worse," said Helen. "I'm more concerned about where Sissy might be."

Jason stopped directly in front of the house and noticed footprints in the snow that were barely visible because additional snow had fallen and nearly buried them. "Stay here for a second. I want to look at something."

Jason got out of the car with his flashlight in hand and walked onto the vacant property next to Sissy's house. He looked at the direction of the tracks and noticed that they seemed to be headed toward a deserted alleyway. He returned to the car where Helen waited.

"What did you see?" Helen asked.

"Nothing. I was just looking to see if there was any sign of Floyd."

"Was it there?"

"No, nothing," Jason answered.

After dropping Helen off at her home, Jason decided to drive back to Wood Street to see if he could find Floyd's tracks and to see how far he could follow them. He parked his car at the end of the alley where he'd seen the footprints. Low and behold, there they were; the same shoe prints where still faintly visible.

He followed them for nearly a mile, and came to dead end. He was about to give-up when he noticed a batch of snow that had been disturbed. Again, there where prints. Someone had made his way into the wooded area that led down over a hillside to a row of old and abandoned commercial buildings.

He made his way down over the hillside and began again to look for the tracks. Jason walked behind the boarded up buildings, looking for any indication that Floyd might have come this way. Up ahead, in the brightness of the morning sun, he spotted a couch leaning against an opening in the back of one of the vacant buildings. There was no snow on the top of the old couch.

Something didn't sit well with Jason as he approached the obviously disturbed area around the couch. What he saw were footprints, the same prints he'd been following. Quietly, he walked up to the opening hidden by the couch. The building was an abandoned warehouse. He'd driven by it many times without really noticing it.

He climbed into an open window behind the couch. He'd entered a small back room leading to a corridor that divided the warehouse into two parts. Most of the roof was filled with holes letting the sun in to expose a number of burnt-out cars. The air was filled with the constant sound of water dripping from the already melting snow that dripping through every hole in the roof.

Jason continued to look and listen for Floyd. He searched every corner of the structure without a sign. Just as he began to think he'd taken himself on a wild goose chase, he heard a distant moan. He ducked behind a pillar and glanced around, looking for a potential source of the moaning. He heard the noise again. It seemed to be coming from a stairwell leading to a lower level. The sound was becoming more and more distinct — it sounded like a man snoring.

He slowly moved closer to the source of the sound. The snoring suddenly stopped, causing his heartbeat to speed up and overwhelm any other sound he heard. He stood still for a moment, being sure not to stumble against anything or make a sound. The snoring resumed, louder than before.

He made his way to the doorway of a room about fifteen feet by fifteen feet that was lit by a couple of candles. There he was, lying on the floor on a stack of cardboard, sleeping without a care in the world. Jason gazed around the rest of the room.

Just beyond the light of the candle he saw six small legs from the knees down to their three pairs of shoes. *Children!* The three of them were looking directly at him. Jason gestured for them to be quiet as he slowly walked toward Floyd. He carefully picked up a piece of two by four off the floor, and without warning struck Floyd on the side of his head with all his might.

The blow woke Floyd didn't knock him out. He quickly got to his feet, just in time for another blow to the other side of his face. Jason threw the piece of board down and gave Floyd a strong kick to the groin as he was falling to the floor. He immediately jumped onto him and used his weight to pin the semiconscious man to the floor. He quickly undid his belt and used it to tie Floyd's hands behind his back.

There were short pieces of rope lying around the room that Floyd had apparently used to tie up his young victims, so he grabbed one and used it to tie Floyd more securely. He then tied Floyd's feet together and hurriedly tied him to a six-inch thick metal support post.

Finally, Jason felt safe enough to pause. He sat back against the wall, still cautiously watching Floyd to make sure he was completely secured. He got back up to his feet and took one of the candles over near the three children, who had began to cry.

"It's all right now," Jason told them. "You're safe. I'm going to take you to your homes."

There were two small girls about five years old and one boy, who looked to be even younger. They were tied together and secured to a support post just like Floyd. The children began to quiet down and cling to Jason as he walked over to Floyd, who had not yet regained consciousness. He tugged the ropes to be sure Floyd wasn't going anywhere.

Jason lifted one of the children onto his back and picked up the other two and held them in his arms. He then headed back toward the dark corridor. With the three children clinging to him, he made his way to an open area where he heard another child's voice.

"Hey," the young girl's voice calmly called out.

"Who's there?" Jason asked.

"It's just me," the child said. "Sissy Williams. "

"Holy God! Where are you, kid?"

"Right here," she said while knocking against a door in a dark corner nearby.

Jason found the door and set the children down. "Stand back away from the door, Sissy," Jason instructed.

He kicked the door open with one thrust, then knelt down on one knee and hugged Sissy. "Don't worry. You'll never have to worry about Floyd again," he said.

"Is Floyd here?" Sissy asked.

"What do you mean? Didn't he bring you here?"

"No."

"Then who did?" asked Jason. "Never mind, let's just get out of here."

He gathered the three smaller children and headed for the only exit he knew — the same one he'd found following Floyd. Suddenly, a garage door slammed shut up ahead.

"Shit!" Jason said. "Listen, don't make a sound. Sit right here. When I tell you to, take the children's hands and run toward that hole in the wall," he whispered pointing at the sunlit opening.

Jason hid himself in a dark crevice as a male voice called out, "Floyd? Hey, Floyd! Where you at, boy?" The man unknowingly walked towards Jason who lay in wait.

"Yo, Floyd!"

The next sound was a piece of wood meeting the head of the man with the loud voice. He was smaller than Floyd and didn't put up much of a fight. The first blow knocked him out cold. Jason gave him second whack, for good measure, just to be sure he was really out.

Jason the second man to the room where Floyd was tied up and was happy to see he still out like a light. He tied the smaller man to the post where the children had been tied up. Once that was done, he returned to the children.

Jason took them out the garage door the second man had come through and found the keys in the ignition of the still running, brand new black Cadillac. He loaded the children into the car and drove them to the near-by West Liberty Police Station. Everyone at the station directed their attention to Jason as he walked through the center of the police station corridor carrying all four of the children.

A female officer walked up to Jason as he got closer to the main desk and lifted one of the children into her arms. "I know someone who's been looking for you, Bobby," she said with a warm smile on her face. "Bring them this way, sir. Where did you find them?"

"Look what we have here. It's Sergeant Barry's missing boy."

"Somebody get him on the phone," another officer said. "Hurry it up! Hey, Bobby, we're glad to see you."

"Where did you find these children, sir?"

"I found them not far from here in an abandoned building. They need blankets and food, but I think they're okay," said Jason.

During the commotion, Jason found his way out of the station and back to the Cadillac without speaking further with the police. No one noticed him leaving. He drove around until he found a pay phone and called Helen to tell her he'd found Sissy.

"Where are you Jason?" Helen asked.

"I'll be seeing you later. I've got unfinished business to attend to. Tell the police I'll come back later to fill out any paperwork they need. Just say

I'll be bringing them two child rapists, though I guess one of them is now a murderer too."

"Where are—" *Click!* The sound of the phone disconnecting came before Helen could finish her sentence.

Jason was headed back to his captives. He had no intention of giving these two men a fair trial! He was going to have the same level of sympathy for them that the rapist had on his daughter.

# CHAPTER 40

Back at the abandoned warehouse, Floyd had just regained consciousness. After a few moments of tasting his own blood, he spotted the Bishop tied to the post where he'd left the three children. His attention was drawn to a dark corner at the other side of the room by a rustling noise in a pile of small boxes.

"Who's there?" Floyd asked, while squinting into the dark area. There was no answer. "Hey!" he shouted as the noises continued.

Suddenly, three big sewer rats came into view. They paused, then two of them boldly stood on their hind legs and looked directly into Floyd's eyes. The others continued to chew on a piece of bacon they'd found somewhere.

"Get outta here!" Floyd yelled and kicked out at them with his bound feet. The rats were startled by his yelling, and stood perfectly still for a few seconds before continuing to scratch through the boxes in search of food.

"Hey, Bishop! Wake up, man! Hey! Wake up!"

The Bishop began to stir and realize that he'd been bound with his hands behind his back and tide to an iron post. "What in the name of Jesus happened here?" he asked Floyd.

"I don't know, Rev. I was asleep and then somebody hit me over the head 'til I passed out."

"You stupid ass! You must've led someone here. You know what that means? The copes are probably on the way here right now. That means you, Floyd — not me — will go to jail for the rest of your life. Do you know what they do to child molesters in prison? You and the rest of them can go to hell!

I'm not going to take a fall for this. I'm gay, I'm not a pedophile. When they find the bodies of those children in here, someone's going to pay and it ain't gonna to be me!"

"Rev, I hate to tell you dis, but you as guilty as any of us. You're da one who take da childrens to da buyers."

"You may be right, but I've never murdered anyone. You're the one, you and your white pedophile friends. I'm not going down with you, Floyd. I'll do and say whatever it takes to stay out of prison, including exposing all of you."

"Why don't you shut-up and try ta get loose."

"Get loose? I can't even move. Whoever hog-tied us like this obviously knows who we are and where we are. And you know they'll find those dead children."

"I don't know nothing."

"That's because you're so damn stupid!" the Bishop said.

"You know Rev, it's a good thing I can't get loose, 'cause if I could you wouldn't be callin' me stupid *ever* again."

"Listen. I hear something. Shhhh."

"That ain't nothin' but some damn rats over there in the trash pile," Floyd said.

"Oh, God! I don't know why I let myself get involved with you or that damned Myers. Oh, Lord, if I could only get out of this one. Never again, I mean never, will I get involved with another child rapist. Oh Lord! Lord, Lord!"

"Shut up Rev! Why don't you just shut up?"

Floyd had a small penknife in his back pocket. While talking to the Bishop, he he'd been trying desperately to get it into his hands.

"Shut up? Don't you forget I'm the one who's fed you all these years."

"Yeah, Rev, you fed me from da money I made for you hustlin' children. Don't forget all da little boys you played wit."

"I never harmed a one of them. You and your sick friends are the ones who killed all those babies. I hope they hang your ass, Floyd. If it wasn't for your stupidity, I'd be at my church where I belong."

As the Bishop continued on and on with his cowardly accusations, Floyd finally got his knife out of his pocket and began to cut through the ropes.

"Oh, God! I can't believe you brought someone here. You idiot!"

Floyd managed to get his hands free and quickly cut the ropes off his feet.

"Oh! Thank you, Lord! You got loose. Get me out of here. Hurry up and cut me loose!" the Bishop demanded.

"You know what, Rev? I decided I'm sick of you and your phony prayin'," Floyd said as he stood over the Bishop. He kicked the him in the stomach, causing him to moan and bend over as much as the ropes would allow.

"Oh, God! He's done gone crazy. Okay, Floyd. Okay, you win. Just help me get loose and I'll make you rich. Just- just get me out of here before they come."

"No, Rev. I think its time for you ta meet yo maker. I didn't bring them kids here, you did. I'm tired of hearing ya flap ya fagot mouth."

"Listen, Floyd, just cut me loose, man. We can beat this. Come on. Help me!" the Bishop pleaded.

"Here's yo help, fagot," he said, and thrust the blade of his knife into the Bishop's stomach.

"No, Floyd! Please don't kill me! Please, Floyd! I'm begging you, man! Please!"

Without another word Floyd stabbed the Bishop again and again. He stood upright folded and pocketed his knife and watched while the Bishop lay panting and near death.

"Hey, Floyd," a strong voice said out of the darkness. Startled, Floyd turned around and found himself face to face with Jason. Floyd's knife was deep in his pocket, so there was no way out there.

Jason was leaning against the doorway with the same board in his hand that had taken Floyd down before.

Floyd smiled and looked directly into Jason's eyes. "What you gonna do, man?"

"You know what I'm gonna to do. I told you before. Your child raping days are over. Have you forgotten that already?"

"I see," Floyd said. "But what's going to keep me from takin' that stick from you and whippin' yo ass?"

"I'm not a little girl, Floyd, I'm a man. Are you forgetting that you only beat on small children?"

"I see." Floyd stood rubbing his chin and looking at Jason's board and back up to his face. "What you gonna do? Hit me with that board?"

"I might. I'm kind of undecided right now. I'd like you to jump at me so I can pay you back for what you did to Sissy. But, on the other hand, I'm thinking I should do the right thing and turn you in to the police."

"I see," Floyd repeated.

"You know what, Floyd? I want to be absolutely honest with you. I have no intentions of turning you in. In fact, I'm going to beat your brains out and leave you here with the rats, including that human rat that you just stabbed. I've never been so calm and sure about something in my entire life."

"I see," Floyd nervously said. The room was cold but sweat had formed on his brow. "I want to turn myself in. I just need your help. You're- you're not a killer. You suppose to be a good man. You ain't like me or the Bishop, or like ole Henry was."

"No, Floyd, I'm just like you. I am filled with rage. I'm going to rip your heart out and feed it to the rats. Look at 'em, Floyd. They seem to know that you're going to be their next meal. Look at 'em! Go ahead. Look!"

Floyd glanced down at the rats. Jason was right. They seemed to be watching and waiting to see what the two humans were going to do next. Their beady little eyes seemed to be pleading with Jason to lay this human trash at their feet.

"Look how many there are, Floyd. A few moments ago there were only three — now there seem to be hundreds."

Jason lifted his board and poked it into Floyd's chest. "What's the matter, Floyd? Does that bring back recent memories of earlier today? You know what it's like to be afraid? Do you know what its like to know someone is about to do you harm, inflict pain, and maybe break your jaw? Or how about I just quickly break your neck?"

Floyd stood contemplating what he should do. His eyes were shifting side to side as he wiped his mouth with the back of his hand. "Okay, listen. I'll admit to what I did. But, I was just as much a victim as Sissy and the others. Henry rape and beat me when I's a boy — he raped me near every day. You can't imagine the hurt he cause me. I was too ashamed ta tell anybody and too afraid ta run away for fear he'd find me and torment me like he did when he was mad. I'm sorry I am like I am. I'm sorry I hurt Sissy. I did it to pay back Henry for what he done ta me. I kept seein' him in her. She look like him. I love Sissy. I wanted her for myself, but she kept lettin' Henry touch her."

"Shut up, you sack of shit! You can pull that pathetic act on somebody else."

"Alright. I'm sorry. There's somethin' in me I can't control, some evil that cause me ta do things I don't wanna do. It ain't me, man. I swear, it ain't me. When I first meet the Bishop, I try ta get him to rid me of da demon. But, instead, he entice me into havin' sex wit him. I'm a sick man. Can't you see that?"

"Yes, I see it, Floyd. I've got your cure right here. Let your demons die here with you and the rats."

"I drank some of dem demons into me. But when I's sober, I never hurt Sissy. Ask her. There was times she was happy I was in her life wit her mother."

"Well, Hazel's dead now, Floyd. You killed her. I know you must have thousands of reasons and excuses why you are who you are. You can't change who you are, Floyd. Accept who you are and take the demon, the drunk, the abused little boy you were, and all that is you with you so God can judge you. I'm not judging you, Floyd. I'm convicting you. You know that no child is safe with you alive. You know it as well as I do. You're giving me the same excuses that every child rapist gives. They're all sorry until they have the opportunity to do it again. Think of the anguish that so many children won't have to go through with you gone."

"Just take me in. I don't want to fight you," Floyd said.

"Oh, we're not going to fight. That would be silly. I couldn't lose because I have every reason to win. No, we're not fighting. Fighting is a sport or a game fools play. Did you know that the walls in this room are twelve inches of reinforced concrete, and that the door I'm standing in front of is solid steel? Did you know that this room was at one time a twelve by twelve safe? It's no wonder no one could hear the children's cries in here.

"No, I'm not going to fight you. I'm going to leave you in here with the Bishop and the memories you have of all the nights you had your way with Sissy. And, oh yeah, the rats. I almost forgot the rats. Look at them, Floyd. They seem to know what I'm saying. The little buggers are jumping for joy. Who knows, Floyd? Maybe you can have your fill of sex with them. I'm sure some of them must be young enough for you."

Jason stepped back and slammed the door shut, just as Floyd ran and crashed all his weight against it.

"Wait!" Floyd shouted through the steel door. "Don't leave me here! I'm a victim, too! I'm begging you!"

"I'll tell you what. I'll come and let you out the moment Sissy says she misses you. Or, hey, the rats got in, maybe they'll show you another way out."

"But I'll starve to death!"

"Eat the Bishop. That's probably something he has always enjoyed."

"No! Please!"

"Please? Did I hear you say please?" Jason asked as he opened the door. "Is that the same 'please' that you heard from that child? You, of all people, should know that saying please doesn't work. Please is just a polite way of asking for something. Don't you remember laughing when Sissy said please? How about another word like stop or you're hurting me, or how about no? All of those words turn you on, don't they? Enjoy yourself, Floyd. All your pervert friends will join you very soon in hell."

"Wait, man, give me a chance. I'm sorry for what I did." As Floyd pleaded he slowly moved toward Jason until he was finally close enough to make an attempt to grab him. Jason took one step back and smashed the board hard against Floyd's head. He then took another step back and slammed the vault door closed again before Floyd could make another attempt.

"Wait! Don't do this. Please!"

Jason threw the board to floor and walked away while Floyd continued to beg.

# CHAPTER 41

Floyd sat in the dark in the concrete room that was previously a bank vault and would soon become his grave. He was locked in with the Rev's dead body. He was alone with that body and about two dozen big rats that had already began to make a meal of the Bishop. A thin line of light barely squeezed under the crack beneath the solid steel vault door.

Floyd laughed in a deep mumbling tone. "Ha-ha-ha, Ole Floyd done got himself in a jam," he said to himself. The blood of Bishop Jones had soaked his clothing, causing him to shiver as he continued to talk.

"I'm not afraid of dying. Lord knows I've lived and prayed as a true believer. Yeah ... I've let the devil lead me the wrong direction more than I should have. But, the bible says, 'Let he who hasn't sinned cast the first stone!' I believe in Jesus. I believe that he died on the cross for the forgiveness of my sins. In my heart, I know I was foolish. Please forgive me, Jesus."

Time passed, but Floyd had no way to know how long he had been inside the vault. It didn't really matter. He was hungry. Rainwater trickled down a cold wall in the corner and had formed a stream that seemed to stop at the pile of old clothes where he'd had his share of sex with his victims. He put the side of his face tightly against the wall and let the water to run into his mouth. Unfortunately for him, his eyes had fully adjusted to the darkness of the room and he could see that his roommates had devoured the flesh from the Bishop's hands and feet and were now digging into the stab wounds.

They seemed to accept the fact that Floyd was a spectator to their feasting. Still, there were always three or four rats standing upright on their hind legs watching Floyd as the others ate, drank and occasionally chased each other.

More and more rodents seemed to be finding their way into the vault. In a couple of days, the flesh on the Bishop's body seemed to just vanish, and more of the rodents began to look at Floyd as their next meal.

The squeaking and squealing was driving Floyd crazy. "Shut up you fuckin' rats! Shut up! Shut up! Shut up!" he screamed as he stood up and kicked at one of the them that had been standing guard. The rat slammed against the wall and landed on the floor, where Floyd stomped it and another that was near by to death. After a few moments of continuous scuffle, Floyd leaned his back against the wall and slid down onto his rump to rest.

The room was totally quiet as he raised his head and looked at the two dead rats that were being sniffed by several of their comrades. He turned his head toward the Bishop, and all the others now stood upright looking directly into his eyes.

One of the rats that were sniffing the freshly killed rats drew his attention up to Floyd and snarled, showing its sharp bloodstained teeth.

"Get outta here 'fore I kill you too!" he yelled as he stretched out his right leg to kick the snarling rodent back away from his kill. In a frantic motion, Floyd picked up of the dead rats and ripped it into two pieces. He threw the head into the crowd of rats. He paused for a moment as if to signify that they could have that piece as a share of his kill, but the rest belonged to him.

He quickly lifted the remaining piece of rat to his mouth ripped into the flesh. He devoured the remains and started on the second rat without hesitation. The remaining crowd of rats stood motionless, watching as Floyd licked the last of the blood from his fingers and gazed up at his newly discovered food source.

One after another, the rats cautiously returned to their routine of feasting. They seemed to know that eventually the Bishop's body would be gone and a showdown between the trapped human and a host of rats was eminent. They would get their turn.

Floyd killed and ate enough rats to satisfy his hunger and then sat back and continued his prayers to God. Every once in awhile he glanced over at the Bishop and the rats that had now eaten out the his eyes. "See no evil, evil," Floyd said and smiled at his own joke. "To tell the truth, Rev, you look better now than you've ever looked. If the rat meat wasn't so good, I'd take a bite outta crime," he said and laughed again at his own morbid sense of humor. "You get it, don't you Rev? "A bite out of crime?"

All the rats seemed to pause at the same time as Floyd laughed loudly. "Bite out of crime, see no evil. Ha-ha. Rev, you always wanted to lose weight. Look at you now!" Again he laughed. "I'm funny, huh Rev?"

Floyd dozed off but couldn't afford to go into a deep sleep for fear the rats might try to get their revenge. So, he slept with one eye open and repeatedly prayed, joked and ate. He reminisced about the many times uncle Henry had taken him down to the boiler room and give him cigarettes while he fondled his private parts. He'd been just seven years old then. His uncle was always so loving and gentle. "Boy, oh boy," Uncle Henry would say. "If they ever find out what I let you do, they would put you in a jail for kids."

For years Henry had taught Floyd how to perform sex acts, while convincing him that it was always his idea. Henry was simply accommodating the youngster. Between Henry's acts and the recently murdered Bishop's homosexual acts, Floyd never knew what a normal boyhood was. Once he became an adult, he knew of no other way to please himself sexually other than what he'd experienced as a boy and throughout his young adult life.

When he discovered his childhood was not normal, Floyd began to impose his own sexual desires on children as soon as the opportunity presented itself. One of his first victims was Sissy Williams, Uncle Henry's four-year-old daughter.

In addition to Henry's daughter, Floyd found himself performing sexually with Henry's new bride, who was twelve at the time of her first sexual affair with Henry and fourteen when they married. Floyd was 16 when he helped the Bishop and his Uncle Henry in the act of disposing of Henry's first wife by strangling her at Henry's request. She'd found Henry sexually molesting their four-year-old daughter, Helen. She'd threatened to expose Henry and his comrades as a child-molesting ring. Henry told Floyd to rape and strangle his wife and make it look like a rape and robbery. If he'd refused, the Bishop and Henry threatened to put Floyd in a local boy's institution.

# CHAPTER 42

The rats had finished eating all the flesh from Bishop Jones. What was once a short plump body was now a skeleton. Floyd had adjusted to the smell of his decomposing victim long before now. The stench from the spoils of the Bishop, along with the rotten smell of the rats, filled the air. But, odor was the least of Floyd's problems now.

The rats had two alternatives. They could attack Floyd and try to eat him or they could leave the vault, which meant that Floyd would die of starvation. Either way, Floyd was doomed. His only hope was that someone would find him and set him free. Jason, the man who'd locked him in the vault to protect the world of children from a calculating pedophile, was the only human being who knew where he was. It was doubtful that Jason would have a change of heart. The only hope left for Floyd was prayer.

Once the final morsels of flesh were gone from the Bishop, Floyd could see the hole the rats had used to get into the vault. He got up from his area and shoved the rats aside as he made his way to the hole. He put his head against the floor and peered into the small. It was only the size of Floyd's fist.

Through the hole he could see the dozens of rats that had run out of the hole in fear of him and an iron pipe that looked like it was about five feet long. He knew the pipe might offer him some hope. *Maybe I can use that to pry open the door.* Floyd immediately reached through the hole trying to get to the pipe, only to be attacked and bitten by the rats.

He quickly withdrew his arm, dragging two of the rats along with it. They had their teeth buried in his flesh.

"Damn it!" he shouted as he shook his familiar foes to the ground and tried to stomp them. He yelled and tried to frighten them away from his pipe. He looked through the hole to see if it worked. They came closer, as if they were waiting for him to feed them. Floyd sat back for a moment contemplating his options. There were none. *I got to reach that pipe or die.*

Again he yelled to frighten the rats away before thrusting his rat-bitten arm back through the hole all the way up to his shoulder. He felt the threads of the pipe with his fingertips, but couldn't quite grasp it. The rats were franticly biting and clawing his flesh as Floyd barely moved the pipe towards the hole.

"You bastards," he mumbled in pain, but didn't withdraw his arm. With one last hard push, he managed to grab the pipe and yank it. Again, the rats clamped onto his arm. This time he managed to bring most of the pipe through the hole and into the vault. He shook his arm, loosening the grip of the rats. They fell to the floor and he again stomped as many as he could.

He grabbed the pipe and pulled it nearly all the way through before it stopped. He pushed and yanked again and again, only to find that a tee section of the pipe prevented it from coming through.

"Damn it! Damn it! Damn it!"

He settled down for a moment and began to bend the pipe back and forth. The end of the pipe suddenly snapped and came through the hole causing Floyd to fall. The rats used the opportunity as a last attempt to take down their huge potential prey. Floyd shook and smacked at them like a man on fire. He slapped them off one after the other as they relentlessly attacked. They seemed to know this was their last chance at Floyd.

He stomped rat after rat and threw them against the wall. He kicked and knocked them away as fast as they came. Finally, they stopped. They gathered on the other side of the room by the hundreds. They seemed to be communicating, and discussing their next plan of attack.

Floyd wasted no time using the pipe to pry the board loose Jason had used to block the path of the door's track. The board sprung loose and the iron door slid open, letting terror back into the cribs of Washington. The child molester/ rapist/ murderer was free.

# CHAPTER 43

The days following the Floyd's disappearance and the death of Sissy's mother found Helen working diligently to legally adopt her stepsister. Her attachment to Sissy had grown overwhelmingly in a short time. Helen could see herself in Sissy, just as she was at age nine — without a mother and yearning for the spiritual affection a child needs to grow.

No one knew where Floyd went. Helen didn't care where he was; she just hoped he would never return. The police were looking for him on a murder and kidnapping charge. Hopefully they'd find him.

Jason knew exactly where Floyd was. Not only that, he assumed that by now Floyd was no longer a threat to anyone since he was entombed in the abandoned bank vault. Jason felt no guilt, after all, he didn't put him there, and he only left him there where he'd violated so many helpless children. He left him there, where justice would be served the moment his last dying breath was expelled.

Floyd made his way back to the house where he'd made Sissy's life a living hell. The house had been boarded-up by the police, and it had been abandoned. Floyd broke through a basement window without being seen. The house was just as he left it, with most of his belongings still in place. More importantly, there was food and water.

After more than a week of hiding and planning of his next move, Floyd began to venture out into the night.

Meantime, over in Arlington, Sissy had been placed in Helen's custody and was preparing to attend her new school for the first time. With Helen by her side, she quickly adjusted to her new life. They both knew that somehow they were going to make it. They knew that happiness had to be just around the corner, even though that emotion was something neither Helen no Sissy had experience much of.

Jason made it a point to stop by and spend time with the two princesses whenever he could. He'd begun to fall in love with Helen. Just seeing her took his breath away. In his eyes, she was a shining jewel. Jason believed without a doubt that Sissy had given Helen a reason to live. Under her protection, Sissy was destined to become the type of person that would leave a positive mark on the world.

In Helen's opinion, Sissy was a gift. Though she was just a child, Sissy seemed to have the ability to project love that didn't require love in return. "Me and you babe" quickly became their motto.

Jason was the one man in their present lives they trusted to provide a sense of safety. When Jason's car pulled into the driveway, there was always a feeling of joy, especially since they both knew that Floyd might be somewhere waiting to take both of them back to that place of fear and cruelty.

Jason had the strength to accept what he'd done to Floyd as a necessary evil; but he, being burdened with morality, experienced a lot of guilt. In his own mind, he reasoned that he really didn't kill Floyd; he'd left him to escape if he could. Maybe *Floyd's not dead. Maybe he escaped and ran off to keep from being prosecuted for Hazel's murder*. Despite all these possibilities, his true hope was that Floyd suffered in fear and met his Maker just as he deserved.

Floyd holed up inside the vacant house on Hill Avenue for another ten days. Each day, he yearned to get revenge for the disruption of his life as a successful child rapist. He developed a special hate for Helen and a lust to get his hands on Sissy once more. As for Jason, Floyd knew that what he intended to do to Helen would satisfy his hate for him. With his heart full of vengeance, he set out to get his revenge.

The sun had set and it was well into the night when got to Helen's house. He carefully made his way through the shrubs without being seen. Peering into the kitchen window, he spotted Helen and Sissy preparing to leave the house. They were talking and laughing as Helen searched for her car keys. Floyd couldn't take his eyes off little Sissy. He couldn't remember seeing Sissy look so happy. Her eyes sparkled as she laughed at a remark Helen made. Floyd found himself filled with desire as he continued to stare at his prize.

"I don't know why I can never find my keys. You would think I'd be smart enough to put them in the same place every day," Helen said with her usual kind smile. Sissy went around the kitchen with Helen, looking under everything movable.

Suddenly, Sissy stopped in her tracks.

"What's wrong, Sissy?" Helen asked. Sissy stood motionless with her head down and an expression of panic on her face.

"What's wrong, babe?" Helen asked again, this time with more concern in her voice.

Sissy looked up at Helen and said, "I don't know. My heart is screaming, telling me to cover my head and close my eyes."

Helen went over to Sissy, reached out her arms and drew her into a tight hug. "It's all right now. You're safe with me. I won't let anyone hurt you again."

Sissy glanced toward the dark window where Floyd was looking in. He didn't move, he just stood gazing into the eyes of his prey. Without warning, Sissy began to scream.

"Ah-h-h-h!" He's here! He's here! He's here! She screamed, while nervously stomping her feet and burying her head in Helen's chest.

"It's all right, baby. He's not here. Don't worry," Helen said in an attempt to calm Sissy down. Helen's own heart began to pound with fear but she continued to assure Sissy.

"No! He is here! Floyd's here! Please, let's go. Please, please, big sister, please, let's go!"

"Okay, just settle down. We're going. I just need to find my keys."

"No! Please, let's just go. Right now!" Sissy screamed as she began to pull Helen by the hand toward the front door.

"Okay, okay. We'll go. Let me just call Jason to pick us up."

"No! Let's get out now. Please, big Sister."

"Okay."

Floyd sat quietly in the dark, smiling at the two frantic females. As they headed for the front door, so did he. By the time Floyd made it to the front of the house, Helen and Sissy had run down the driveway and onto the street.

"Damn!" Floyd said from the darkness as he watched them walk out of sight. "Damn it to hell."

In Helen's haste she'd forgotten to lock the front door. Floyd calmly lit and smoked a cigarette in the dark. He sucked hard enough to light the front of his upper body, revealing the face of an evil man with mayhem on his mind. He pulled the cigarette down to his side to tap off the ashes. Holding his head toward the heavens, he let out a stream of smoke. Then, of course, he walked the front door that Helen had left unlocked.

Once inside, he searched for and found Helen's keys. Floyd tried the keys in all of the locks. Finding one to the basement door he removed it from the ring. He put the keys back where he'd found them; hoping Helen wouldn't discover the missing key.

He left the house, leaving the front door open, just like he found it. Floyd anticipated that Helen would return with either the police or Jason. He returned to his hiding place outside and waited for his prey to come home.

Within an hour, Helen and Sissy returned with the police and Jason, just as Floyd had expected. He watched at a safe, undetected distance as the house was searched and declared safe. After the police left, Jason and Helen calmed Sissy down and patiently assured her that Floyd was nowhere near and she could safely go to sleep. They stood watch over her and talked well into the night.

"Well, it's time I say good night," Jason said to Helen. "Don't hesitate to call me if you see anything out of the norm."

"You know I won't. I'm beginning to think I don't want to go another minute without talking to you even if there's nothing wrong," she said.

"There's something I want you to have. I'm not comfortable with this idea, but I'd rather be safe than sorry." He handed Helen a semi-automatic

.25-caliber handgun. "I know you don't approve of weapons but you and Sissy's safety may be in jeopardy. Hopefully, you'll never have to use it."

"I don't even know *how* to use it. Even if I did, I couldn't kill anyone, not even Floyd."

"I know, but listen to me. If Floyd is still alive and in this area, I suspect he'll come after Sissy. He has nothing to lose. I hope he's left this town or even better, he's dead. I'll know for sure by morning. For now, take the weapon just in case. It's fully loaded and ready to fire. I'm going to put it under your pillow. You don't have to touch it unless there's no choice."

"Okay Jason, but what do you mean you'll know by morning?" she asked.

"I can't say right now, but I'll explain as soon as I can." As Jason began to turn away from Helen, Ozz, much to his surprise, found himself influencing Jason's mind, so he turned back around. Ozz wanted Jason to speak some of the words he had in his heart. Ozz's affection for Helen had grown far beyond his dutiful obligations. Helen had bloomed into a pure and breathtaking woman. Love, to Ozz, was a connection of souls, an instinct to protect, or a passion for heaven's spiritual hands, but with Helen, something had taken him to a whole new dimension of desire.

"Turn around," Ozz's thoughts demanded while he stood in Jason's path and motioned as he had seen humans often do. Jason paused as if someone was trying to tell him something.

"What?" Helen asked. "Is anything wrong?"

"No, nothing's wrong. I just suddenly felt like I have more to say. I have an impulse to stand before you and express some well-hidden feelings that I have for you. I'm not good with words. I've always been a man who holds my thoughts of romance in a place inside of me that no one else can find. I feel so awkward when I try to bring my feelings to the surface and express them in words."

Helen stood facing him. Nervously, she stepped a little closer. "I've felt your boyish expressions of affection before," she said, "but there's something about this spontaneous approach that's weakening my ability to stand here before you."

"I'm sorry, I didn't mean to—"

"No, please don't be sorry. It's just that the strong feeling of love that I have for you has grown into something I've never felt before."

"Can I hold you in my arms for a moment?" Jason asked as he reached for her and gently drew her in.

"Please, hold me," she responded as she moved as close as she could get. He tightened his arms around her and stroked her back.

"If anything were to happen to you, I'd cease to exist," he whispered. Helen held her head against him and breathed in the essence of the only man she'd ever longed for. She'd known him for years, always wanting to hold him and melt into his body. She'd restrained herself, only to find the fire growing each time they shared the same space. Her intuition told her that she and Jason were true soul mates. The only step that hadn't been taken was her desire to yield to her own lust and beg the man to make love to her. She often longed to grab hold of him and not let go until she reached the bliss that only he could bring.

"It's inevitable that fate somehow brought us together. You do know that, don't you?" he asked.

"Yes, I know it. Please don't let fate take much longer. I can't make it. I need to swallow you up with my passion. If it doesn't happen soon, I will simply die of a yearning heart," Helen said.

"Just hold on, baby. We'll get our turn. You're too amazing for our consummation to be anything less than perfection. I, too, am bursting with desire each time you given me the kindness of your precious smile. We've never been intimate, but we have made love a million times."

Ozz found himself in a trance and made an attempt to return to his angelic state of mind. Jason pulled back away from Helen and briefly kissed her on the lips. He took a deep breath and delivered a few clumsy words. "I'll talk to you in the morning."

Jason knew he had to go back where he'd left Floyd to die. He knew he couldn't leave that question unanswered. Did Floyd somehow escape? he wondered. *Did Sissy actually see Floyd? Did I put Sissy's life in danger again by not taking Floyd's life when I had the chance?* He had to finish the job.

After he left Helen's house, Jason stopped at his home and picked up his 9 mm. Jason was as brave as any human could be. He also knew how to be afraid. Floyd was truly the type of man to fear. Floyd's type have no fear of pain or dying. His type had no reason to be alive anyway, so they don't fear death. To men like that, life is only a place they did not choose to come. *Floyd needs to be put to rest, and I'll be the one to do it if he isn't already dead.*

Jason parked his car just outside the warehouse and made his way inside the perimeter fencing. There was an eerie feeling of evil in the air. There was also a smell of death that hung like the smog around some of the old factories down along the Ohio River.

He used his flashlight to illuminate what the moonlight couldn't. Finally, the vault door was just ahead. Jason experienced bout of fear as he pointed his light at the board he'd used to block the door. It was still in place, just as he'd left it. He pried the board loose and slid open the door enough to enter.

The smell inside was overwhelming. He raised his shirt and covered his nose and mouth in an attempt to block the stench. The flashlight showed a frightening view of the Bishop's skeleton. Chill after chill ran through Jason as he kept his back to the door.

He slowly moved the light around the room to where he'd left Floyd. *He's not here!* His level of fear accelerated. Jason cautiously looked up and down the empty corridor and back into the vault. He moved the light around the room searching for Floyd's remains. For a moment, Jason thought he'd spotted the Bishop's skeleton again. As he quickly moved the light back and forth, it revealed two skeletons. Jason sighed with relief. Even the stench didn't hinder the good feeling of knowing it was over for Floyd.

He locked the light onto the skeleton he assumed was Floyd's. *I thought it would be a lot bigger,* he thought. He stepped back out of the vault and slammed the door shut for what he thought would be the last time. *There's no need to brace it shut. Floyd has raped his last victim.*

\*\*\*

Back at Helen's house, Floyd deiced he'd waited long enough. Like a deadly serpent, he quietly used the key to let himself into the basement. He knew exactly where to find his helpless prey. Both Helen and Sissy were fast asleep. The day had been long and tiring for them. The emotional highs and lows had taken their toll and they were both sleeping deeply.

Floyd had no problem sneaking into Helen's room without waking her. He closed the bedroom door quietly behind himself and approached her bedside. Kneeling down, he positioned his face just inches away from Helen's and stared at her. Her beauty didn't impress him in the slightest.

As he watched her sleep as if she had nothing to fear, Floyd's rage made him to breathe harder and harder. This made Helen stir in her sleep and brush her hair from her forehead. Floyd decided to play with his prey by blowing onto her face. Again, she stirred without waking and wiped her nose with her finger.

He grasped the blanket that was lying just below her neck and slowly pulled it down, exposing her scantly clad breasts. Again, he blew on her. This time along the bottom of her neck, down onto her breasts and then back up to her lips. She gasped slightly to regain her breathing rhythm and continued to sleep, not knowing that she was about to die.

Jason had made it to his home and decided to wait until morning to reassure Helen and Sissy that Floyd would never be a threat to either of them again. He wouldn't be able to explain how he could make such an assurance without revealing the part he'd played in the death of the two men. He chose to keep his secret to himself. He lay back on his bed fully dressed and within minutes, fell into a deep sleep.

Ozz was in a state of panic. With the powers of heaven, he watched as Floyd toyed with Helen as she slept. He also knew that Floyd had no intentions of stopping with Helen. His plan from the start was to punish Helen and to have his way with Sissy. After that, he had no plans. He intended to look no further at life. He was less concerned about how he was going than who he was going to take with him.

Ozz was fully aware of the capabilities of this evil man. He was aware of Floyd's intentions of pleasing himself with Sissy for the last time. Ozz knew that Floyd, like all cowards, could kill with ease as long as there was no real threat to himself.

*Wake up!* Ozz shouted with his heart. *Wake up, Jason! The one you love is about to die. Jason, wake up!* The angel wanted to pound on Jason's chest to let him know about the danger. There was no way he could communicate with this human. *Maybe I can touch his heart without taking his life.* With that thought, Ozz used every ounce of emotion within him to reach the Jason's heart. *He's going to kill her!* he shouted once more before taking his hand and touching Jason's heart for a split second.

Jason felt an explosion of pain in his chest and sat up coughing and panting for air. "My God," Jason said out loud, "I had a nightmare like no other in my life. I dreamed Sissy pushed her finger into my heart. I wonder if she's all right." He glanced at the clock. It was 3:30 a.m. —he'd only been asleep for an hour.

He decided to call Helen and have her check on Sissy. He dialed the number and let it ring. It rang and rang, but there was no answer. He called again. The ringing of the phone startled Helen out of her sleep, and she opened her eyes to find Floyd looking right into her face.

She tried to scream but Floyd had already cuffed his hand tightly over her mouth. She began to writhe and kick, she realized she must fight or die. She couldn't free herself from Floyd hold, but she did manage to kick the ringing phone off the hook.

Jason was relieved when he thought Helen had finally picked up the phone.

"Hello?" he said into the receiver. There was no answer, just muffled sounds that sounded like scuffling coming through the earpiece. "Helen?" he shouted, "Are you alright?" There was no answer. "I'm coming over there! I don't know if you can hear me, but I'm coming over there to make sure you're all right!"

He slammed the telephone down and headed for his car as fast as he could.

Helen did all she could to free herself, but Floyd was too strong. Within minutes she'd passed out from lack of oxygen. As her body went limp, Floyd loosened his grip. He wasn't ready for her to die — he hadn't had his fun yet. He ripped the sheet into strips and tied Helen to her own headboard. Once she was bound to his satisfaction, he stuffed pieces of cloth into her mouth to keep her quiet.

He then headed to Sissy's room. The closer Floyd got to her, the more she was disturbed, even in her sleep. By the time he reached the door to her bedroom, she was sitting up screaming for Helen. "He's here! Please, help me! *He's here!*"

"Of course I'm here. You knew ole Floyd was comin' back to get his girl. You knew that, didn't you?" He quickly walked to her bedside before she could escape. He grabbed her, first by her kicking foot and then by her hair, nearly yanking it from her scalp. "I'm going to fuck you 'til you die right in front of yo sister. So shut up," he said while he violently dragged her from her room and into Helen's.

Helen was beginning to regain consciousness. "I'm, glad you're awake, bitch, 'cause I want you ta see how a *real* man takes what he wants. I'm gonna let you watch and then I'm gonna snap yo neck like I did your momma's."

Ozz was frantic. He struck out at Floyd but nothing happened. He wished, he prayed, he howled his frustration. He tried everything to help Sissy. The beast was impervious to his actions. Then, after a slight pause, Floyd slowly turned and looked right into Ozz's eyes and said. "You can watch, too, you Holy piece of shit."

Ozz looked startled and Floyd continued, "What? You think I don't know 'bout you? I knew you when I was bein' raped. You got no strength. You're just meek and harmless. If I had time, I'd fuck you, too." You can only hear prayers — you're useless."

Ozz tried with all his might to do some kind of harm to Floyd, only to see him continue to rip Sissy's nightgown off and throw her onto the foot of the bed at Helen's bound feet.

"Helen? Helen!" Jason shouted as he began to beat on the front door. "Let me in!"

Suddenly, Floyd's attention was drawn to the noise downstairs. At the sound of Jason's voice, he quickly moved over to the front window and saw that Jason was alone.

Floyd grabbed the .25-caliber pistol Jason had left for Helen and hurriedly unplugged the lamp. He then went out into the hall and unscrewed that light bulb. He waited there for Jason, who was now kicking in the door.

When it gave way, it swung open and crashed into the entryway wall. The house was dark and quiet, and Jason yelled out again. "Helen it's me. Where are you?" He drew his 9 mm from where he'd tucked into his belt and held it up to his chest. He again called out Helen's name. There was no answer.

He slowly moved toward the stairwell while listening for any sound that might indicate that Helen or Sissy were in danger. The door leading to the basement had been left open. He walked along the hall feeling his way as his eyes adjusted to the darkness. Peering down the basement steps, he reached in, found the light switch and turned it on. Cautiously, he descended the stairs. Suddenly he heard Helen screaming upstairs.

"Jason! He's waiting for you!" Floyd got back to her and quickly stuffed the rag back into her mouth. With that done, he returned to his trap.

When Jason heard Helen's voice, he recklessly ran toward the stairs with his gun in hand. Without caution, without fear, he leaped to the top of the stairs. Once at the top, he realized there were no lights and not a sound. Jason realized he might die right here in this house.

"Helen?" he shouted. "Where are you?" The hall was in total darkness, but he could hear Helen and Sissy making warning noises like someone had gagged them. "Helen, I'm coming in. As for you, Floyd, I know you're here and this time I'm going to kill you. This time I'll leave no doubt. You hear me, boy? *I am going to kill you.*"

Jason felt along the wall, trying to find the light switch, while looking in the direction of Helen's room where the muffled noises were still coming. He dropped down onto his knees and slowly crawled along the floor with his gun leading the way.

Floyd stood silently, laying in wait. He really wanted the opportunity to shoot Jason without the threat of being shot himself. In the dark, sweat rolled down Floyd's face as his cowardly streak began to show itself. Jason's taunting and threats were beginning to work.

Floyd could vaguely see the dark shadow of Jason crawling towards him along the hall floor about 10 feet away. He pointed the .25-caliber semi and smiled to himself because Jason had unknowingly crawled right into his sights.

Jason looked up in time to see the first spark from the barrel of Floyd's weapon. Floyd fired five times, each shot hitting Jason and moving him back until he helplessly slammed into the far wall. One of the shots struck Jason's throat causing him to wheeze as he gasped for air.

Floyd's courage returned when he realized Jason had become another kill for him. "Uh-huh, now what you got to say 'bout that, mister hero? You ain't talkin' so loud now, are ya?" He walked up to Jason in the dark and kicked him as hard as he could. There was responsive.

Ozz had watched as Floyd emptied his gun into Jason. "I've got to act. I've got to act now. Please, God Almighty, take my life instead of his. Don't let that animal win again."

Ozz kneeled down and positioned himself against Jason's bullet riddled chest. "I won't just watch this time or ever again," he said and Jason heard.

As Jason was about die, he felt himself being held by Ozz. He had no way of knowing who it was that held him so dearly. "Please help them," Jason whispered. "Let me die, but please help them."

Ozz was now squeezing Jason tightly and rocking him back and forth like a child. "You're not going to die," he said.

Ozz turned and looked up at Floyd, who was about to kick Jason a second time. Ozz turned around and faced Floyd and unexpectedly felt the full force of Floyd's kick. In pain, Ozz fell backwards onto Jason. He became aware of Jason's 9mm lying near his right foot. By the dim light of the moon shining in through a window, Floyd also spotted the gun at Jason's feet.

Still slightly afraid, Floyd cautiously bent over to pick up the weapon. Suddenly Ozz used the last of Jason's strength to swing his right fist into

Floyd's face. The blow sent Floyd onto his back as he continued to fire his weapon at Jason until it was empty and began to just click... click... click...

With Ozz's help, Jason managed to reach out and pick up his 9mm off the floor. In one miraculous move and with all of Jason's remaining strength, they leaped onto Floyd's chest before he could regain his advantage. After a brief struggle, Ozz maneuvered Jason's body completely on top of Floyd.

With both men trying to gain control of the weapon, Ozz painfully and slowly moved the pistol against Floyd's eyebrow. He was boiling inside as he thought of the torment and misery Floyd had caused Sissy. In complete anger, it was Ozz instead of Jason who found himself moving the tip of the pistol tightly against Floyd's left eye, "This is for little Sissy." Without mercy, he thrust the barrel of the gun into Floyd's eye socket and with another thrust the barrel penetrated as deeply as it possibly could into Floyd's brain.

In a fraction of a second, Ozz bid Floyd a final farewell, and after one final thrust, he pulled the trigger three times in succession. Before the gun made a sound, Floyd screamed like a squealing pig, "Oh, God!" Then, the three explosions blew his brains onto the floor and surrounding walls.

Ozz and Jason quickly stood up and weakly leaned against the wall. They watched as Floyd's body jerked and convulsed in its death throes. Ozz felt Jason's face frown without pity as he fired again at the devil. Each shot lit the hall as the bullets drove Floyd's body further and further away.

Finally, it was quiet and it was over. This time the clicking sound came from Jason's gun. After a brief pause of complete silence, Jason reached up to his neck and felt the blood pouring down onto his chest. Ozz, too, felt the warm blood of the human trickling down his forearm as he looked at what appeared to be his own arm clothed with Jason's bloody shirt. Together they looked back down at Floyd's bullet-riddled body and clicked the trigger a few more times before losing consciousness and slumping to the floor.

## CHAPTER 44

Four days had passed and Jason still lay unconscious in the trauma ward at Mercy Hospital. Helen had been at his side night and day. She gently held his hand as he slept. Jason felt his eyes rolling, but his eyelids stayed shut. He tried to squeeze Helen's hand to let her know he was okay, but that didn't work either.

Jason began listening to a faint voice he'd never heard before. The female voice was mellow at first, then quickly became crisp and clear. "Never in all my being have I been a part of an act so gallant. Before you, there has only been one who chose to dwell within man rather than remain in God. He, unlike you, made his choice as a stand against man and God. I bow my head to you Ozz. My compassion and all of my wishes are and always will be for and with you on your journey to come.

"However, just as you were warned, all of your angelic knowledge will be lost to you for eternity. But your spirit will never cease. As long as the innocence of a child is at risk, your inclination toward protectiveness will remain in the hearts of good men. Just as evil has spread itself, so, too, will your gallantry and goodness spread. As long as it is God's wish, we will be at your side."

After a long pause she spoke again. "Your dissent will not be in vain." With those final words Chism reached down and stroked Jason's brow. "My brave but foolish hero, for your willingness to sacrifice your own life you will be exalted in the heavens like no other before you." At Chism's tender touch, Jason ascended to heaven and Ozz took his place.

"My name is not Ozz," he softly said, as he suddenly and consciously found himself looking at Helen as she sat gazing him.

"Well, look who has rejoined us," Helen jestingly said as she embraced Jason.

"You'll never know how glad I am to hear your sweet voice. The doctors said, it would be a miracle if you pulled through, but I knew you'd make it. I just knew it!"

For the first time in his being, Ozz felt the warmth of woman's touch. He'd always known of his love for Helen, but never had he dreamed such a union could be possible. Yet, here he was, being held by the woman of his dreams.

"Did you hear her?" he asked, as he looked around the room.

"Hear who? Sissy and I are the only ones here."

"Oh... I guess I was dreaming. Is Sissy all right?"

"Ask her yourself, she's been sitting in this room with you since you were brought here and she refused to leave until she knew you are all right. She insists that you've become her guardian angel. In a strange way, I understand why, because you're my angel, too."

Sissy slowly walked up to the bedside, leaned down and put her head onto his shoulder. "I'm so happy that you'll get well. I thought he'd taken you away from us," she whispered.

"No one will ever take me away from you, no matter what they say or do," Jason, or was it Ozz, said.

"Just be quiet and rest. You've got a lot behind you and even more ahead."

## *The End*

## Author's Note

Every child is entitled to protection from predatory adults. The question is who is responsible for their safety and well being? The answer is the mother and each member of the family. There is or should be a long list of loving people who step up with a devoted willingness to assure a child's right to remain innocent. These protectors should insure this, even to the point of giving up their lives.

The so-called pecking order should also include each and every real man that has an ounce of courage or pride in his manhood. This man can be a father, an uncle, a brother, a neighbor, a stranger, or a friend. To all who will not stand, there is an obvious conclusion that he is certainly not a man.

To every man and woman of any age, every hero, be he or she real or imaginary — no being has the right to turn his wrath on a helpless child. For those who have managed to reason that any act of violating a child can be acceptable, I can only say this: As long as you are alive, may your soul burn, and thereafter, may your soul burn for eternity.

www.ingramcontent.com/pod-product-compliance
Lightning Source LLC
Chambersburg PA
CBHW052028070526
44584CB00016B/1948